THE TWO WAY STRETCH
Modernism, Tradition and Innovation

ROBERT MAXWELL
ACADEMY EDITIONS

Attempts have been made to locate sources of all photographs to obtain full reproduction rights, but in the very few instances where this process has failed to find the copyright holder, apologies are offered. Unless otherwise stated, all images are courtesy of the author: p10 (right) Le Corbusier Foundation; p12 (right) Benedikt Taschen, Cologne; p17 (left) Prestel, Munich; p19 (right) St Martin's Press, New York; p33 Abbeville Press, New York; p63 (right) Tim Street-Porter (Esto)

First published in Great Britain in 1996 by
ACADEMY EDITIONS
An imprint of

ACADEMY GROUP LTD
42 Leinster Gardens, London W2 3AN
Member of the VCH Publishing Group

ISBN: 1 85490 438 8

Copyright © 1996 Academy Group Ltd. All rights reserved. The entire contents of this publication are copyright and cannot be published in any manner whatsoever without written permission from the publishers.

Distributed to the trade in the USA by
NATIONAL BOOK NETWORK, INC
4720 Boston Way, Lanham, Maryland 20706

Printed and bound in the United Kingdom

CONTENTS

The Dialectic of Positions	6
Positive Futures: The Lure of Technology	23
Positive Futures: Re-animating the Old	44
The Loss of the Absolute	54
The Wisdom of Uncertainty	66
Growing Up in Great Britain	77
Notes	95

THE DIALECTIC OF POSITIONS

■ I have long been fascinated by speculation about the forces acting on the individual in the moment of artistic creation. Although we are all part of a shared tradition, it is a tradition that is never complete and fixed, but undergoes continuous change. We are just beginning to be aware of the mysterious process by which innovation occurs and the tradition is extended. Everything produced by the individual owes something to the society to which he belongs and from which he takes his cultural framework. Yet the individual by his own efforts can exceed what society accepts, not necessarily by a great deal, but by enough to set up a space of movement, a space into which culture itself will eventually expand.

In the Western tradition we are used to according a special value to the rebel who, after being rejected of men, is found to have bestowed insights which extend our culture. Jesus Christ may be said to have invented this role. The artist, in particular, is valued in this way, to the point where the stereotype of the avant-garde artist comprehends the idea of a potent personal vision. To begin with, this vision is apparently rejected, but something of it is accepted and in due course this becomes part of the common fund of values. Without the independent experimentation that only the individual can propose, society would be lacking in fresh ideas. It is through the integration of individual efforts that society extends and renews itself.

Western culture seems more than any other to extend itself solely through confrontation. Indeed, change through confrontation seems to be culturally normal within the three great monotheistic religions; or is it the climate of the Eastern Mediterranean that is the ultimate cause? There seems to come into being an enjoyment of the tension that an individual of talent arouses in seeking to change some aspect of culture. This tension is a burden he must bear, in steeling himself to overcome the resistance his ideas will surely meet. At the same time the sense of purity and danger that surrounds the breaking of taboos provides the individual with an exhilaration that can make the effort seem worthwhile.[1] It is by no means easy to change culture in even a small respect, yet this is now the aim of every artist who wants to be considered part of the avant-garde. The process of inducing change and renewal is for the individual an honourable destiny, but it is now itself institutionalised *as a process*. Our society no longer regards the *status quo* as anything but a chance state of affairs, a transitory condition of an unknowable story. We now anticipate change and try to influence it to our advantage.

Culture owes a debt to every artist who has helped by struggle to change it, and in the West the aura of Christ is extended to the artist who has the vision to project a redemptive value. I am thinking here especially of our European culture, the growth of which has become more evident through the conscious effort of building the European Community. If it seems so far to be overburdened with bureaucracy, this may be because the role of saviour at a political level is currently politically incorrect. This effort is of course directed at changing political and economic institutions, yet it also calls for a change in consciousness, and in this area the contribution of the artist can be as important as any other. The goal becomes nothing less than the construction of the future. Such a goal is evident in the way the artist entered into the reconstruction of Europe in the years after World War I and the Russian Revolution. The avant-garde artist took up the redemptive challenge, and art became virtually a substitute for religion. Today this has progressed to the point where the museum has almost become the alternative site of spiritual renewal.

At the turn of the century, HG Wells, author of *The Shape of Things to Come*, coined the phrase 'the cybernetic world state' to describe a future world government that would attempt to harvest all the benefits of progress while avoiding catastrophe. The future would then be managed in the interest of the survival of all. The League of Nations, the United Nations, the World Bank, the World Food Organization, and so on, are steps in the gradual evolution of a world-view that would instigate a policy for the benefit of humankind. Ineffective as they are, overburdened as they are by bureaucracy, these institutions mark the beginning of the attempt to apply social engineering to the project of managing the future, a project that can clearly only be effective if applied at a global scale. What effectiveness they may have, in terms of support and collaboration, is entirely due to our perception of the future as fraught with danger as well as with promise, and this perception of danger only bites at the scale when the future is equated with the prospect of the world becoming uninhabitable. The space between danger and promise, precisely the zone where the radical artist attempts to work, is fast becoming of concern to all.

Danger and promise in turn call up propositions that answer to a belief in the values to be maintained, and to reasoning about how this is to be done. There is a dialectic between reason and belief that is now manifesting itself at the global scale. Reason alone, however, is an insecure foundation, and the idea that we have reached the level of wisdom where we are even *capable* of managing the future is hard to accept with equanimity. Reason on its own creates utopias that are abstract and rigid, a source of nightmare, as we see in Hilberseimer's theoretical cities. In a parallel movement, the exhilaration of the expressionist artists in the Weimar Republic, or in the young Soviet Union, quickly turned to nightmare, as authority stepped in and sought to control and manage the effervescence produced by the intellectuals. It was not until later that Karl Popper warned us that social engineering was a dangerous procedure because of the unexpected side effects it engendered.[2] We are still fixated by the success of hard science and technology, and find it difficult to grasp the complexity, not only of nature, but of culture.

The diversity of European culture is hardly less complex than the diversity of global culture and I think it is evident that after centuries of development presided over by the compulsion of innovation, we are today as concerned to conserve as to innovate. At the global scale it is no longer possible to ignore the problems that innovation has brought with it. As the biosphere on which we depend for life comes increasingly under threat from human exploitation and population growth, it is no longer possible to regard the world as a field to be unthinkingly exploited. This surely applies not only in the economic sphere but in all aspects of human endeavour, and this must include art and architecture. Attitudes direct motivations, art expresses attitudes; architecture expresses attitudes and implements the results of those attitudes in technological terms. Changes in attitude, once absorbed by society, are implemented decisively and to the extent that they consolidate error, their potential for harm becomes intensified. What the lone individual can change by an effort of taking thought is not balanced by the efforts that must be expended by many in order to save the world from its own excesses. Once a *form* is accepted and institutionalised it resists further change, especially if it carries an economic advantage for a whole class of people.

To recognise this is not to justify a blanket conservatism. Rather, we need to acknowledge that the situation is essentially dialectical in nature: man proposes, society disposes. Every thesis generates its own antithesis, and the synthesis that society imposes is itself transitory and ineluctable. There is a continual process whereby forms are displaced by new forms. I subscribe here to the formulation proposed by the German sociologist and cultural critic Georg Simmel, for whom the invention of new *forms* is the only evidence by which the forces in society can be made visible to us, providing the trace of what we have done that informs us of what we have become.[3] This accumulation functions both as record and as occasion, as a compendium of values and as a provocation to create new values. Through creating new forms we forge the future, but every

LEFT: Le Corbusier, Algiers study, 1938; RIGHT: Le Corbusier, The Hilton, Honolulu

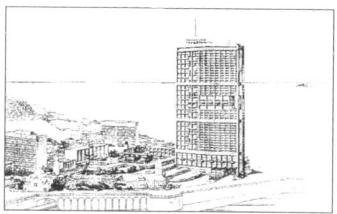

form, once defined, must take its place in a procession, must be ready to be displaced by another.

This process whereby the new is absorbed and used up was well described, thirty years ago, by the architect Emilio Ambasz, while he was a teacher at Princeton University.[4] He stipulated that the new form does not arise *in vacuo*, but only by reference to the existing. He saw a process where the new, the *prototype*, deferred to an existing ideal, the *archetype*, before being absorbed into culture as a *type*, involving a more or less useful life as currency, as convention, only to decline into a *stereotype*, facile and shallow, losing in power and credibility, ready to be abandoned. We exist in a dialectical space between innovation and the recuperation of values.

In this view tradition and innovation are mutually necessary. Each one of us may have a preference for one at the expense of the other, but it is impossible to adopt one to the exclusion of the other because both are part of the same process whereby society maintains continuity while allowing change. As Wittgenstein proposed, well before the advent of modern semiology, tradition only endures by the efforts we are prepared to expend in order to renew it. We are suspended between past and future, neither of which do we truly know, but only as hypotheses, as interpretations. It is this space of action into which the artist must enter in order to create the new.

An artist like De Chirico, with his ambiguous attitude towards the past, sees the incidence of abstraction and rationalism in innovation, while recognising that the result is a kind of Frankenstein. An artist like Goya sees the humanity in the human animal, but recognises also the horror of his uncontrollable impulses. Recent events in Ireland, in Bosnia, in Algeria, underline the dilemma: belief cannot accept an alternative view. To expel disbelief, the only clean solution is to eliminate the infidel. The frenzy of killing is an attempt to wipe out doubt, since belief is too insecure to tolerate dissension. Belief thus becomes a *casus belli*, but without some sort of belief we become material automatons. Neither past nor future, reason nor unreason, bring a secure answer: we are destined to experiment, to make mistakes, to court disaster, in oscillating between reason and belief.

For this reason, we swim in a sea of questions, knowing that there can be no easy answers, even for the lone artist, and especially within the essentially public art of architecture. Architecture can never be weightless, can never be totally abstract. It finds itself, as an art, uneasily placed between the freedom offered by Abstraction and the duty of Representation – that is, of reflecting accepted conventions by which meaning is maintained. This is why Adolf Loos denied public architecture the freedom of self-expression, except in the case of a tomb or monument. Architecture must defer to the social but this does not mean that it must totally succumb to convention. To keep it level with the challenges that arrive every day, we still must depend on the individual architect who will take a chance, risk opprobrium and propose new things. The compromise that he must make to have his ideas realised sets up the movement by which they will finally be at least in part accepted. What we should not expect, however, is to legislate in order to have our particular world-view written into the laws. This only creates oppression and gives strength to the inevitable reaction. We recognise that the process of renewal is continuous but not smooth. Each creative individual has to fight dragons and

LEFT: Reichlin & Reinhart, project for house in Vezio, 1975; RIGHT: Same image upside down

search out the source of tyranny. Every system which fixes values in the interest of its own prolongation becomes tyrannous and this extends to economic systems that supposedly work for the benefit of all, but certainly work for the benefit of some. The tyranny of the market is as much in evidence in the field of cultural innovation as it is within economic realities.

For this reason, too, I interpret the dialectic of new and old as a complex one, for within the new there is still something of the old, which precisely renders the new recognisable; and within the old the new is already pregnant. I have tried to find a visual analogy for this double relationship by presenting Reichlin & Reinhart's project for a house in Vezio twice, once upside down. If we look carefully, we can see the Post-Modern in the Modern, but also the Modern in the Post-Modern. In the same spirit I have written a book with the title *Sweet Disorder and the Carefully Careless*.[5] Some creation is possible by, as it were, letting go, abandoning oneself to a sweet disorder; some only comes by taking pains, by a careful effort that must then be concealed. In creative work there is a dialectic between reason and intuition, between control and abandon, and each mode of work requires the other. Neither is secure in itself. In experience, sweet disorder is part of the sensation of living, while the carefully careless is a construction that goes with the critical act. But let us remember that every artist is also his own critic.

The professional critic is also to an extent an artist, if an artist in words, and he can only be parasitic on the work he professes to criticise. The job of the critic is to help explain original work, and aid its assimilation into society. The critic, however, often betrays his deep envy of the artist, and, lacking the assurance of an originator, tries to back one attitude against another. The critic is even more loath than the artist to be labelled *reactionary*. A critic does not risk very much in coming out for one side, as his words are soon forgotten anyhow. And just as he finds it easier to favour one position over another, so too he tends to ignore the complexity of the field where the dedicated artist operates – a field where the careful distinction between sweet disorder and the carefully careless may be a secret source of both weakness and strength. The space between the two positions tends to dissolve, the closer one looks: which was the greater artist – the apparently spontaneous Louis Armstrong or the immaculately well-arranged Duke Ellington? Both were artists of the first magnitude. When British jazz broke up in the early sixties, two positions emerged: Ken Colyer, who worked through jam sessions and followed the path of *sweet disorder*, and Chris Barber, who worked through careful arrangements and followed the path of the *carefully careless*. What seems to operate, in conditions of uncertainty, is a dialectic of *partis pris*, a clarification of positions by means of opposition. The dynamics of *either/or* are easier to grasp and more convincing to the undecided, than the synthetics of *both/and*. So for a critic who wishes to enter the ambiguous space in which the artist operates, all the interest must lie between the extremes, and an explanation for the strange history of modern architecture must also be sought in that ambiguous realm.

Modernism, the attempt to create a rational future, was prepared in the Enlightenment, created anguish throughout the nineteenth century and came to fruition in the twentieth century; and the twentieth century was understood to be itself an opening to the future. Le Corbusier had no doubts that the imposition of the Voisin plan would save Paris from suffocation; today, it is difficult to imagine that it was intended in all seriousness. What was sweetly rational at the scale of the individual building became a Frankenstein at the urban scale. If it had been built, and if we had lost Paris, we would still have to deal with the same high levels of pollution caused by automobile exhausts. And Paris would be an artificial and universal system, a tyranny close to a nightmare.

Within the present world view, which still owes more to structuralism than to deconstruction, we are caught between the forward and the backward view. The present is all too obviously imperfect, and must be criticised in the light of a theoretical construction, that is some form of ideal. The ability to criticise society by reference to something outside only became possible after the growth of travel in the seventeenth century opened up other societies and made possible the comparative studies that formed such an essential part of the Enlightenment. By the nineteenth century, with the growth of social studies, it was inevitable that social engineering should come into being as the attempt to make science reflexive, that is, to apply science to mankind. This then raised the question posed by Nietzsche as to whether man could impersonate God and make good the deficiencies in creation, due either to sin or accident. Utopia becomes a means of criticising the status quo. But Utopia is a projection, a sort of mirage, limited by the ideas of its moment. The ideal can never be realised in its own terms, and the empirical cannot have a meaning unless it reflects the ideal to a degree. In the work of almost every architect of importance within the history of Modernism, we can distinguish certain aspects that are innovative and others that are reactionary. There is a temptation for the critic, wise before the event, to side with innovation, which is more likely to be the winning side than the known and the familiar. Whether or not the future develops as hoped is hardly important; what is important is to be seen to be on its side. However, this tendency to side with the future is also in itself a form of rhetoric. No one will notice, probably, if our projected future does not come to pass, and who will care? Better now to be grouped with the angels, by adopting the dynamic, anticipatory, position.

In the general context of a technological society, the benefits of progress are thought of as self-evident, and it is true that technology has already brought material progress, especially at the level where the individual life is affected. Yet this is no self-evident progress, but one fraught with doubt and misunderstanding. Part of the legacy of modern science is the need to deal with uncertainty, a problem that preoccupied Einstein for thirty years after he went to Princeton. Uncertainty, we now know, is not limited to particle physics, whether at the level of infinitely small particles or at the fringes of our observation of the sensible universe. It attaches itself also to all attempts to explain ourselves to ourselves, to analyse the medium that sustains us. Positivism, once offering certitude to science itself, is now suspect in the culture of science. In cultural studies, it has become a divisive issue, separating conservatives who wish above all to recuperate moral values from progressives who want above all to eliminate false consciousness. In particular, the uncertainty in the very use of language which has been pointed to by Derrida and others emphasises the conditional and indeed improvisatory nature of our 'truths'.[6] Truth may be fugitive, but the limitations of language still permit us to achieve positive results that change society by applying linguistic and mathematical models to empirical experience: the scientific method.

The scientific method operates by a process of making hypotheses that can be incorporated in physical experiments, and either confirmed or denied by observation. In Popper's terms, confirmation is sufficient grounds for proceeding further, but is not a final result, it is not the final truth. No final truth is required for success, each stage of understanding is strictly conditional, and the scientist has no problem with that – as a scientist. In the three centuries since Francis Bacon first defined it, the scientific method has accomplished a whole series of revolutions in understanding the material universe and, by the applications that follow through technology, in achieving material progress. Measured in population growth, prosperity and extended life expectancy, this progress is no illusion.

Yet, though material progress seems to be a given condition of modernity, it does not lead to a state of saturation, when everything has been explained and accounted for. Rather, the more that is learned about the constitution of the material universe, the wider are the horizons that remain to be explored. As explanations become more complex and speculative, a sort of metaphysics re-emerges, the universe becomes remystified. This is evident in the popular reception of Hawking's *A Brief History of Time*, where physical phenomena hypotheticised *in extremis* take on a mystical aura. In Hawking's terms the Big Bang account of the beginning of the universe invests physics with a benign mystery without directly invoking a Creator, and without explicitly refusing the profane value of secularisation. A similar compression attaches to time as viewed in the other direction, looking to the future. It expands indefinitely but contains within itself the possibility of its transformation. The future is perceived as always on the verge of a miracle, a breakthrough to a different state of being. The effect of this is to make the future of the present very different from the future of the past. Progress is no longer simply a gradual amelioration of conditions, but an approach to a magical threshold. This dynamic results in a perennial interest in the latest thing, and (as Gianni Vattimo has said in his book *The End of Modernity*) in 'affirming the new as the fundamental value'.[7] Technological progress does not point to an end, rather to an indefinite future, but this future begins to take on a mythic dimension.

Belief is intolerant, but ideology, which cannot dispense with an element of belief, is also intolerant. Modernity, as ideology, cannot tolerate a transcendental belief in values outside of reason; yet without that reference point it takes on the febrile nature of a pursuit of the impossible. Every discovery, every new thing, has a limited shelf life. In Simmel's terms, each new form is destined to be supplanted by another, in a sequence

LEFT: Women Bathing, 1906; RIGHT: Revlon advertisement, The most unforgettable women, 1990

that has no end. In this framework, each latest thing brings a momentary relief, and the desire for the latest thing takes on the quality of a search for an elusive resting place.

In the world of fashion, for instance, we respond instinctively to an image of our times, seeing it as sharing in an unknown future; but we reject the equivalent image of a bygone age as futile. Our view of the future now is different from their view of the future then. To see our contemporary images as already futile requires an unusual degree of self-effacement, or possibly of a useful morbidity. Yet the physical reality of the body, which underlies the changes of fashion, is relatively constant and allows us to empathise with the *now* of past times. The fashion designer knows better than the public the unyielding reality of the body, even when reduced to the skinny body, and has to work at inventing a new look to impose on it, in an attempt to redefine the boundary between the Naked and the Nude. Photography completed the de-mystification of the body in movement, which in turn affected the ability to re-mythify the body. Yet the echoes of an artistic style still hang around Muybridge's studies of the naked, as opposed to the nude. The attempt to cancel out the convention of *the nude*, and substitute it for the unadulterated truth of simple *nakedness*, is at the heart of the idea of modernity. But the cancellation of this space of ambiguity brings with it a secular future in which belief becomes more and more attenuated, and as Nature abhors a vacuum, other ideas demanding belief slide into position.

Fashion provides the most obvious case of the game of affirming the latest thing as the fundamental value, cycling and re-cycling the human body through the dynamics of cultural consciousness. But the artist is better at expressing the inherent ambiguity of this in-between space, the mixture of joy and resignation which make up the modern religion of *Stoicism*.

We long for the fabulous, as in De Chirico's depiction of *Perseus and Andromeda* (1940) and wish that our myths were still believable. The hunger to have something to believe in produces strange behaviours: the sighting of friendly UFOs, the conviction that Elvis Presley is not dead, belief in our lucky number in the lottery. But what we experience more often is the inability to attach our private situation to a mythical story, leaving us in a state of pure loneliness with a sense of emptiness, as in Edward Hopper's *Hotel Room* of 1931. This is the modern condition, where secularisation has taken command, and where whatever of the truth remains, it is always incomplete and contingent.

However, the loss of mythical power in our secular life is not complete: the old images are devalued but they still beckon. In the enormous archive that our culture has bequeathed to us we constantly find aspects that can be re-animated. Every instant in our history is capable of being reviewed, of being seen in a new light. It is in the archive that the artist delves in order to come up with something new. Moreover, ritual is not dead, only displaced. The ritual of the crowd still attaches to sport, to political demonstrations, to conventions, to every enthusiastic audience, to the Sunday morning crowd at the shopping mall or at IKEA, to hotel atriums and department stores, to swimming pools and sandy beaches. TS Eliot pointed out, long before Claude Levi-Strauss, that culture includes not only the 'cultural', but everything hallowed by ritual. Consider the list of things he named as outlining the English culture of his time:

LEFT: De Chirico, Perseus and Andromeda, 1940; RIGHT: Edward Hopper, Hotel Room, 1931

> . . . the reader must remind himself, as the author has constantly to do, of how much is here embraced by the term culture. It includes all the characteristic activities and interests of a people: Derby Day, Henley Regatta, Cowes, the twelfth of August, a cup final, the dog races, the pin table, the dart board, Wensleydale cheese, boiled cabbage cut into sections, beetroot in vinegar, nineteenth-century Gothic churches and the music of Elgar. The reader can make his own list. And then we have to face the strange idea that what is part of our culture is also a part of our lived religion.[8]

This list anticipates in a striking way the essays in the first section of Roland Barthes' *Mythologies*, issued nine years later in 1957, which deal with topics as diverse as *The Romans in Films*, *The Face of Garbo*, *Wine and Milk*, *Steak and Chips* and *Ornamental Cookery*. It anticipates the studies of popular culture initiated in Italy by Renato del Fusco and in Canada by Marshall McLuhan, and in this country the interest in popular culture that underpinned the work of the artist Richard Hamilton and the architectural thought of Reyner Banham and the Smithsons. Popular culture was suddenly seen as a sort of base or underlying layer that contributed by its very spontaneity to the definition of culture as a whole. The wide range of the things named by Eliot also reinforces Georg Simmel's idea of the nature of the *forms* that make our culture visible to us. From this we can hazard an idea of the deep-seated changes in culture that act in some way to shift the attitude of a whole population, as in the current momentum of the *politically correct*, which is clearly not simply the product of a few university departments, but resonates widely.

Eliot is not politically correct by today's standards. He talks about culture as an aspect of civilisation, as part of what it means to be 'cultured'. He talks about how we may 'improve our culture', what the role of the élite is in society, the relation of élite to class, regional identity, and about cultural deterioration; all subjects that, if not taboo, are today to be treated with circumspection. In spite of this evident conservatism of a rather old-fashioned kind, there is a certain fascination in seeing the degree to which his thinking converges on issues that would later become re-defined through the development of modern social anthropology and semiological analysis. I believe he is right when he identifies culture as stemming from belief, and expressing itself through *a whole way of life*.

In addition, Eliot speculated in an interesting way about the balance of forces that come together in a living culture. The culture is analogous to language, in that it is beyond social control. Yet, as we have seen with Fascist governments in our century, it is not beyond the power of government to distort culture and endanger its future. The balance of forces may even be precarious, at certain moments of the political process. This sense of the fragility of culture opens him to a dialectical account of it. He sees a constant tension between the advantages of freedom, as the ultimate sanction of a democracy, and the need for order and the rule of law, as the mark of a civilised society. But each aspect brings a danger:

> The danger of freedom is deliquescence; the danger of strict order is petrification.[9]

Eliot attributes the coherence of a culture to its power as the expression of *a whole way of life*. In this he comes very close to the analysis of culture offered by Raymond Williams.[10] Before the development of modern critical studies, says Williams, it was normal to view culture in one of two ways: either as the outward expression of an informing spirit, as in Burckhardt's account of the Italian Renaissance; or as being an epiphenomenon, the resultant of a complex of unknown material forces that come together to produce a whole social order. He carries on to suggest a third view of culture, which we may describe as a *formalist* view, because it treats culture as performing a regular function in social intercourse, analogous to De Saussure's treatment of natural language. In this view culture constitutes a means of communication, because it is systematically coded. It is the system of underlying beliefs and unspoken assumptions that are shared by everyone belonging to a common culture. Because this system underlies behaviour and is unspoken, it is practically invisible. Yet it is the means by which those who share in a culture know *what is going on*. Williams describes this view of culture in the following terms:

> [It] . . . sees culture as a signifying system through which necessarily (though among other means) a social order is communicated, reproduced, experienced and explored.

This view of culture helps to make more credible the idea that changes in the cultural milieu come by stages through the initiatives introduced by individual effort. The accumulation which culture embodies represents both an enormous inertia, and a rich and fertile source of modulation. Since the culture is changing, yet constantly retaining a broad accessibility to all who share in it, it permits both change and stability. In this way, it acts in a way analogous to language itself. To change the language is beyond the scope of a single individual, yet group behaviour on the fringes can and does lead to change in the language. The change is not immediately visible, it may take a generation to produce an effect. Yet, over time it becomes obvious. We can still read Charles Dickens with pleasure, but we no longer speak like Dickens. And Shakespeare is still performed.

This view of culture allows it to be of a complexity that

resists complete formulation. We enter the realm of uncertainty simply because it is impossible to give a complete account of it. We see the reality of this complexity demonstrated in Ernst Gombrich's essay *In Search of Cultural History*,[11] where he shows that nothing in cultural history can be understood through simplification. This understanding can only be achieved by penetrating the superficiality of the myth; yet there is no depth of analysis that can realistically mirror *all* the factors known to be involved. This is a limit of language which concerns only the aspect by which its narrative mirrors that of 'reality'.

However, allowing this complexity to be beyond our assimilation does not mean that we are powerless to act on it, any more than acknowledging the complexity of the sub-conscience makes it impossible to live. We simply do not expect to *exhaust* the argument or achieve certainty. Since culture changes through a dialectical process, we have the freedom to swing on our point of departure and await the repercussions. In analysing it, we do well to remember that the future is always surprising; but also that, under the layers of materialistic behaviour, myth is still alive.

POSITIVE FUTURES:
THE LURE OF TECHNOLOGY

■ More powerful than the ancient myths is the present power of science to change life and work miracles. I recently benefited from a lens implant after a twenty minute cataract operation, made possible only by the invention of the laser; restoration of sight was almost Biblical in its immediacy. Technology brings benefits in many practical situations that directly affect the individual, chiefly by way of certain medical procedures that were once hazardous but are now routine. From dental engineering to hip replacements to fertility drugs, the individual has direct experience of the benefits of progress.

It is hardly surprising that medical technology is subsequently endowed with a near mythical power and even tends to be seen as all-powerful. It is only a matter of time, we believe, before a remedy for cancer is found, and the secret of AIDS revealed. There are no physical problems that will not eventually give in to the scientific method. In spite of Nature's amazing ability to side-step our dispositions – as with the development of strains of microbe that are resistant to antibiotics – we believe that, in due course, these difficulties will be overcome. If there are unexpected side effects, these too will succumb to our powers of analysis. In our desire to re-invest our myths, we turn to this efficacy of applied science, and accord it a status that exceeds its limitations. From being a dependable resource, it becomes a sort of surrogate for the ancient certainties. Technology operates at the point where science has actual power over our lives. With power comes glamour, and we submit to glamour. It is only a step away from mythicising technology.

The pace of technological development is such that it forces change upon us even in the minutiae of our daily lives. When World War II began, the reproduction of music in the home required a special piece of apparatus which was in the course of being transformed into a conventional part of the furniture: the electric gramophone was giving way to the radiogram. Then came music centres. Then came modular music centres, a series of black boxes, an assembly that insists on being a special piece of apparatus, not a piece of furniture. No one under ninety now has a radiogram.

On active service in India, I was accompanied by an old wind-up gramophone on which I played 78 speed wax records, using steel needles. It was primitive, but perfectly appropriate to life in a tent. Then came bamboo needles which could be re-sharpened and did not wear out the wax. Then came the sensitive balanced pick-up head and records which played less violently at 45 and 33 revolutions per minute. Then came tape recorders. Then came videos. Then came compact discs. Then came CD Rom and everything digital. To keep pace with improving technology, we have had to change our domestic equipment several times.

From this follows a desire to be always level with the new possibilities, to be where the state-of-the-art is. This is partly the simple desire to remain socially competitive, but it is also a horror of being on the shelf. Besides, progress brings genuine gains. I remain an indifferent typist, but the word processor takes the pain out of my typing errors, and multiple print-outs take the pain out of carbon copies. Leon Krier used to enjoy pointing out that many architects who considered themselves 'modern' preferred to live in traditional houses; but he himself, an avowed traditionalist, apparently had no problem with owning a car. A car, given the life we lead, is simply a convenience, not an article of faith. Since I first started driving a car (a Morris Minor, 1956) there has been a smooth progression each time I replaced it with a new one, and now when I engage bottom gear I think of the advantage of having synchromesh; and when I change down a gear, I remember the bore of having to double de-clutch my old army truck, and bless technology. However, I still prefer a manual gearbox to automatic, because it gives me more tactical choice, and so the act of driving for me is not so very different from what it was forty years ago. The car is not so different, it is the road markings that have changed – change came in easily assimilated steps

In fact, car technology progresses steadily, but without too much calling in question the investment already made by car owners. A lot of improvements have been made since the days of the Model T Ford, but, like the bicycle, the configuration is essentially unchanged. In the sixties, when I first started teaching in the United States, it was always amusing, each autumn, to read the ads for the following year's automobiles, and notice how a large part of the hype consisted of promoting a new 'look'. Changes in styling were preferred to changes in the technology. There were improvements, but the result looked more different than it actually was. The way that the 'look' of the future can keep us waiting for it is one of the ways by which the comforts of the status quo can be conveniently prolonged.

Engineering design seems to prefer evolution to revolution, and the need to maintain a steady flow in the market is clearly a concern for the manufacturer. We remember how the revolutionary and potentially more efficient Wankel engine was quietly allowed to fade away. In the field of energy management, we notice how few resources have been made available for the development of tidal energy installations, or wave energy apparatus, or renewable energy crops, all of which, if successful in reducing the demand for fossil fuels, might seriously affect the oil market. We have become aware of the need, under the capitalist system, to refresh demand without dislocating the market, and equally to ensure that routine products like light bulbs or nylons will have to be routinely replaced, according to a precise statistical probability. The life of the product is designed along with its market. What ideally suits production is to boost demand without having to re-equip the factory, a process which is most clearly displayed in the area of fashion and the language of garments, and is also visible in architecture. And we are aware finally of the increasingly important part played by market research and advertising in the capitalist project of matching product to market, which in its search for economic efficiency clearly approaches the more general concept of social engineering.

Technology is the process of applying new insights from science to practical life. As science does not stand still, but is driven on by sheer intellectual curiosity and a continuous effort of discovery, technology too is constantly on the move. Unlike science, technology is driven at least in part by the commercial advantages of being ahead of a new market. However much market forces tend to hold on to existing advantages, innovation is still necessary if manufacturers are to reap the commercial benefits of scientific and technological discoveries, even if it requires changes in people's habits. Competition is the incentive to stay ahead.

With an entirely new product, the additional cost of production must be met by a planned sales operation. In other words, a new market has to be developed along with the product, and the whole system would not come into being without being able to count on a certain social cohesion which manifests itself in consumer enthusiasm. For success, the market must be carried along in step with the new possibilities, so that it will in turn sustain the new product. Fashion writers and critics of architecture are two of the intermediary agents of change, helping to make the New exciting and acceptable. It is acceptance of the product that guarantees the necessary numbers, providing a happy situation for the manufacturer and the designer when the product 'catches on'.

This point in the process still marks a somewhat vague threshold, stemming from the mysterious relationship between the individual and the group. From the manufacturers' point of view, it is necessary to mount a campaign, to spend money on publicity. From the consumers' point of view, the band wagon must already appear to be rolling when we jump on to it. For the success of a product, there has to be a perception that we cannot afford *not* to share in the advantages of the

New. A novelty for the few soon snowballs to become a trend that cannot be refused. This usually involves a positive social aspect, the enjoyment of joining the club, and of being with-it. Think how the telephone has developed over the last few years: first the touch-tone, then the mobile, then the cellular phone. To sell the product, a new behaviour has to be sanctioned. The touch-tone phone has brought the doubtful advantage of having to listen carefully to a recorded message, and press *one* when required: the company saves time at the expense of the individual. The cellular phone has changed ideas about privacy: the conventions of phoning in one's car, in the train, from one's restaurant table, or from the street have come into existence as a necessary aspect of the new technology, a behaviour that quietly disposes with the taboo against exposing private affairs in public (a public that, in the event, neither knows nor cares). Nevertheless, these innovations have introduced a real change in the conventions of social life. They have also opened the door to new kinds of crime, as the information highway opens up to street life and hackers match their own ingenuity to that of the invention.

It is evident, then, that our materialistic lifestyle, obsessed as it is with state-of-the-art possessions and tactical social advantage, is still imbued with a certain broad trust in the idea of progress, in the idea that the future will always be better, that problems will disappear. The discoveries of pure science, achieved in the laboratory, have implications for the material future, but it is in the realm of technology that the applications of new science become part of life. These changes are real and many are clearly of benefit, at least to those who can take advantage of them. A measure of this is provided by the statistics for life expectancy at birth and the increasing pace of world population growth. Potentially, a growing population is a growing market, and it is economic growth that provides the key to improved expectations. However, no one as yet has any idea how the equation combining growth in world population, sufficiency of the food supply, agricultural capacity and ecological balance, is going to stand in even fifty years from today. It is not clear that all the new behaviours called for will be of equal benefit to all. Technology and management are together aspects of this development, looking between them to change social expectations and bring behaviour into a new equilibrium. The advance of technology has been a history of overcoming problems, step by step, until in the end a different equilibrium is attained. In this process of trial and error, some problems are solved, others simply go away, and yet other problems appear from nowhere.

There is a gap between the popular idea of a better future and the reality that eventually appears, and this gap is the site of ideological projection. We want to believe in the future, the more so that we cannot any longer call on the gods from the past. An enormous part of our daily experience is involved with the projection of change, and the determination to reap the benefits of the New. The links sometimes seem frivolous, but this does not diminish their importance. Think how Courège drew inspiration from the Apollo moonwalk, and note how for a long time a recurring theme in women's fashion journalism, along with the far out and the exotic, was the call for clothes to facilitate movement and contribute to the success of the 'modern' woman. Women's garments are a long cry from astronauts' suits, but the pull of the new is like gravity – difficult to resist. We want above all to identify with the next stage, to be 'hip' as opposed to 'old hat', to be cool as opposed to naff.

The game of influencing expectations is important: it opens a broad opportunity for everyone concerned with the play of social preference and taste, and so we find a kind of complicity appearing between the organs of commercial publicity and the media in general: newspapers and magazines, fashion journalism, mail order catalogues, credit card promotions, prizes and lotteries. The appetite for being up to date enters social life by a multitude of paths, by way of entertainment, lifestyle, cars, clothes, gossip, restaurants, recreation, sport and a good part of more serious pursuits that define the state of the culture of culture: music, theatre and the arts generally, and this includes architecture – all areas in which new attitudes can be expressed, a market developed and the future prepared. All this is good fun, providing we remember that those who introduce new technology into the market place are never disinterested. In the fine arts we can detect a delicate balance between the work of artists who welcome the new as a stimulus and those who warn us against the state of the world that is coming about. The radical artist makes full use of this ambiguity, combining a positive appetite for breaking the rules and extending the domain of art with a sort of candour that feeds our existential angst and makes us aware of loss.

Architecture on the whole suffers from being treated as a manufactured product, as if it were but one more product offered for sale. This treatment ignores the essential difference between the products of mass production such as cars, which after being designed and tested are sold by thousands in virtually identical units, and buildings, which are more or less unique assemblages of products that have virtually no identity in themselves. There is no theoretical reason why identical buildings should not be spread around just as telephone kiosks are, and wartime prefabricated houses were. This idea was central to possibilities of standardisation that were very popular in the aftermath of World War II. As yet, however, this has not happened. The explanation must come from two points in the materialisation of a building that confer on it a literal uniqueness: its time and its place. Both time and place are unrepeatable in an exact sense, and militate against indefinite reproduction of identical units. Buildings, in other words, are sensitive to context, and in some sense cannot be severed from it.

This dependency of architecture has intervened in the attempt to produce buildings as if they were nothing but the flexible part of a market-oriented process. A building can project a future style of living, but it must do this in one confined site which ties into the existing city or countryside and forms part of a land use pattern determined by existing land rights, and by bureaucratic as well as market forces. This land use pattern has so much common interest invested in it that it becomes difficult to change except in part. Because of this embeddedness, architecture is relatively a slow starter. There is not much of an opportunity to exploit repetitive sales, rather a chance to register popular approval and gain success, maybe eventually repeating commissions. Perhaps because of this, the architect trying to materialise the future acts within a sceptical situation that tends to dramatise the confrontation and increase his paranoia, and as a result the ideological aura surrounding such buildings is intensified. Allowing for the factors that restrict expression in the individual building, it must be said that the impulse to side with future success is as strong in architecture as in other modes of expression, so long as we see architecture as a mode of expression.

However, there are inhibitions against perceiving architecture as simply a mode of expression; it used to be the mother of the arts, and it still hankers after a higher position. A problem arises if we wish to believe that architecture is not so much a mode of expression as an integral part of scientific advance; not science as such, perhaps, but part of science, and with the same principles. In that case the architect views himself as following a path of discovery which has nothing to do with the expression of an attitude, but with the uncovering of an objective necessity, as inevitable as the laws of nature within which science and technology operate. In the development of modern architecture, a strange conflation was made between abstraction as an aspect of art, and the abstraction which allows science to advance by reducing problems with powerful models. Modern architecture adopted the abstract language of art but assumed that this visual language automatically provided a scientific grasp of buildings as shelter. Rather than claim the freedom of expression that the abstract artist assumed, architects preferred to speak with the authority of the scientist, whose discoveries go behind desires to base themselves on an understanding of natural law.

We may doubt whether this decision to follow a path of strict necessity was adopted for any other reason than to be able to claim the cloak of science. The evolution of social life follows rules, not laws of nature. In this area, fashion is more powerful than logic, symbol is more powerful than fact. Attempting to apply the laws of nature directly to an area of everyday life is a doubtful project – a project that encompasses in practice too many steps to substitute a pure scientific process, which is supposed to be free of short term motivation. Concomitantly, an everyday confidence in the power of fact is as much due to belief as to reason, a condition that is nowhere more evident than in the way confidence affects share prices. This was the kind of confidence that underlaid the doctrine of *functionalism*, an important part of modern architecture throughout the twentieth century. Modern architecture, as projected by Sigfried Giedion, Nikolaus Pevsner and Henry-Russell Hitchcock, was to reveal the New, not through introspection, but through the discipline of *following function*. In the event, 'following function' became a matter of following rules, not laws. Rules are man-made, compounded of fact and belief. A compound of fact and belief, of logic and hope, is precisely what we mean by an ideology.

The ideology of functionalism, which was discovered and named around 1920 as a procedure and a style, had the great appeal for architects of releasing them from artistic responsibility. They did not have to justify the forms they used as arising through introspection or the exercise of a sensibility; these forms were seen as simply the natural consequence of logical thinking and scientific facts. They were accorded an objective status. Smart thinking, not fine feeling, was the source of the New. Architects could appeal to an empirical reality as something which *required* a particular outcome, and that outcome was beyond question.

After three-quarters of a century of functionalism, it has become apparent that function has been largely identified with the appearance of function – another case of wish fulfilment.

Function is one thing, the look of functionalist architecture is another. In Britain alone, the look of functionalism changed over the years: Classical Modernism, the new Brutalism, the new Empiricism, the new Historicism, the glamour of High Tech mechanisms, and today, of expressionist curves, have in turn changed the look. But the claim was always to insist that how it looked was how it had to be. With the High Tech architects in particular, this tone persists today. Get the facts right and the outcome will automatically be right. The outcome is always justified in terms of meeting a programme, satisfying a need, solving a problem, helping people. On the public platform, the High Tech architect speaks only of people, never of style. If the result is stylish, this is apparently determined by factors outside of architecture proper, never by way of a preference of taste. We are used to the excessive claims made for novel products, which, however, are readily subject to verification. With buildings, the verification becomes impossibly expensive, and excessive claims go beyond sales talk and begin to smell of hypocracy.[12]

In Britain, especially, this approach has been successful, because people are not happy to think of architects as artists, or of architecture as an art. Most people prefer to regard architecture as a branch of technology and for it to be entirely justifiable by empirical reasons. I have observed this prejudice not only among ordinary folk, but especially among cultural mandarins, whose familiarity with the free behaviour of artists perhaps makes them uneasy about freedom of expression running rampant among those who are asked to design their buildings. In so far as the architect is not doing what he must, he is behaving irresponsibly. To be following a whim or private intuition in the spending of other people's money is hardly to be justified. To be following a vision is only all right if it is not a private vision. Yet, it must be obvious that in key designs like Foster's Hong Kong and Shanghai Bank, image is more important than economic reality.

As image, the building projects the power of the institution

Sir Norman Foster & Partners, The Hong Kong and Shanghai Bank, Hong Kong

and its capability to endure. It therefore projects the future, and with that, the unknown, as the future must be. The unknown casts a spell and the very freedom from convention spells freedom in general, and the power to take that freedom. It is this image that the owner paid a lot of money for. It is an image generally helpful to a bank, above all in generating confidence. Where, in the fine arts, the quality of strangeness appears to emanate from the artist's introspection, in High Tech architecture it cannot afford to admit to such a personal source: it must emanate by necessity from a condition of society, and this is then crystallised as the future, a source that can only be approached by employing scientific insight; a source which then justifies the strangeness it brings, not in terms of personal expression, but as a form of group confidence. By this identification, the architect can continue to produce strangeness, as artists do, but in the name of function. He can remain radical and be part of a continuing avant-garde. The High Tech style aims to blind you by science, but it battens on expectations of the future as a form of Hope. A future is projected that has the aura of the ideal.

Although modernity may in principle be held to have been initiated in the rationalism of the Enlightenment, its development throughout the cultural framework of the nineteenth century was convoluted and uneven. Whilst there were important discoveries in the sciences, there was confusion and contradiction in the arts. This was evident in 'the battle of the styles', broadly an opposition of Classical propriety and Gothic sincerity. The Palace of Westminster – Classical in layout, Gothic in detail – is the clearest witness to what we might term eclectic schizophrenia. In many respects it represents a description of the British attitude towards art.

During the nineteenth century the cumulative effect of the writings of Ruskin, Pugin and William Morris gave the advantage to the Arts and Crafts Movement and the use of vernacular forms was in general conducive to a more adaptable and flexible method of building suitable for the expanding middle classes. Even Edwin Lutyens, who by the thirties was identified with the late Classicism of the British Empire, began his career with some wonderful houses in a more or less medieval vernacular. By the end of the nineteenth century Adolf Loos could point to the English as pioneers of a more practical and liberal lifestyle in clothes and houses[13] and Muthesius could publish an important book on *The English House*. A British architect – Charles Rennie Mackintosh – had an important influence on the development of an Arts and Crafts Movement on the continent: the Art Nouveau in Brussels and the Secession in Vienna. At this point Britain seemed to Continental eyes to be way ahead, indeed close to the United States of America in bringing modernity to a tired old world.

At the beginning of the twentieth century there was much speculation about the need for a twentieth century style of architecture. The periodisation of different styles throughout the history of architecture suggested that each age had a different character, that each age should have its 'own' style. Art Nouveau was a first attempt to identify a modern style. It did not last long because it was soon seen as concerned with decoration and surface, and as such only an elaboration in visual terms of the advantages already gained by the Arts and Crafts Movement. By referring to medieval models, that movement had shifted taste towards a more informal and flexible system, and had made it possible to point to structure as itself a source of beauty – as in spiders' webs, snail shells and medieval barns, and in the writings of Lethaby and D'Arcy Thompson.[14] So functionalism, when it began to enter the rationale of Modern architecture was closely related to ideas of Gothic sincerity, of exposing the underlying truth, of shedding 'mere' decoration in favour of a deeper necessity. Thus the wish to be modern was translated into a myth of Modernism.

However, a structural architecture that bore comparison with medieval models is not altogether new, hardly satisfying to those who saw the twentieth century as breaking into entirely new ground. Another concept arose to respond to that desire, and that was the concept of space. Unlike structure, which had to obey laws of nature, space was more malleable, more conceptual, more metaphysical, perhaps belonging to man rather than nature. It could be argued that a new sense of space gave rise to an entirely new way of seeing things. Space became the other component of the new concept of functionalism and starting as it did in a frenzy of speculation about the existence of a *fourth dimension*, it was more or less mythical from its onset.

The organisation of space is, like structure, an integral part of architecture: it is the useful void that shelter provides, at every scale from igloo to cathedral. One can point to key moments in the development of a rational use of space, such as the change from a row of rooms arranged *en suite* to rooms accessible off a corridor, as used by Vanbrugh in Blenheim Palace; or the emergence of the staircase from corner cupboard to central axis, as in the Baroque. The concept of space that entered into modern functionalist theory was not so much a result of use and custom, as a consequence of perception. Space was seen as a positive quality that could be given character and meaning, that is, become in itself a source of aesthetic enjoyment.

This transformation was due mainly to the German art historian August Schmarsow, who in a publication of 1893 proposed a conception of space as aesthetic object, and as such the essential property of architecture. Schmarsow had been trained by Theodor Lipps, who was largely responsible for an 'empathetic' view of architecture, in which the observer would respond to the *feeling* engendered by an impressive space, such as a Gothic cathedral. August Endell's exposition of Lipps's ideas was widely received, but it was still tied to the idea of construction. Schmarsow made the essential step of abstracting space from its envelope and giving it special properties of its own. This idea was immensely influential with architects, who saw themselves suddenly in possession of an exclusive property. Berlage said 'the aim of architecture is the creation of space, and the space is the essence of architecture'. By 1941, when Sigfried Giedion published *Space, Time and Architecture*, the concept of space as a field of perception had become part of the myth.

The building which sets out not only to be modern, but to project a modernity that reaches out to the future, must be above all functional – the residue of 'functionalism' – but still imbued with ideality. The visible signs of this adherence to principle must show in the crucial aspects of *structure* and *space*.

In the act of building, it is the structure that provides the basic framework, and that both symbolises, and is, necessity. Most High Tech buildings expose their structure as the essential aspect of their nature, and in doing so celebrate the structure as an aspect of truth. Structures made of steel and glass were from the beginning of the Modern Movement considered the most direct expression of modernity, combining the twin aspects of functionalism: the structure reduced to the bones and made visible, space 'freed' by the transparency. But there are certain practical aspects of building that militate against this clarity. Building regulations applying to all but the smallest buildings require that the structure be protected against fire, and the cheapest way to do this is to spray the steel with a protective material. At the end of this operation, the steel cage looks like a chicken loft. To restore the smooth surface that goes with technical precision, the structure has to be further encased in another sleeve, usually a casing of light metal in aluminium or stainless steel. The result is a complex operation, which is neither cheap to carry out nor aesthetically consonant with exposing an underlying reality. It is not a stripping down, but a building up. Even when the structure to be revealed is the actual concrete frame that does the structural work, it must be highly finished, at great expense, so as to match the smooth surfaces and perfection that perfect control requires. So a sophisticated High Tech building is rarely the most direct result of practical necessity, but an elaborate artifice that speaks, often eloquently, of a necessity that has been invented.

All these comments apply very clearly in the case of the Pompidou Centre, where the structure you see is not the naked steel, but an elegant sheathing that is thicker and more monumental than the actual structure which it protects. In contrast, the Eiffel Tower reveals the naked steel of its structure, although covered with layers of paint. The Eiffel Tower is not a building for occupation, and became a national fetish long before modern building regulations for fire protection were drafted. It is ironic that the crowds that ascend the Pompidou Centre by escalator to take in the view of Paris now exceed those who ascend the Eiffel Tower by elevator.

The reason that the Pompidou has so much structure is that the architects wanted to have large floor spaces uninterrupted

Piano and Rogers, Pompidou Centre, Paris

by structural columns. This was necessary so that the building could be said to be 'flexible' – that is, ready for unforeseen possibilities of use – and also because only extensive space has that feeling of being free from obstacles and interruptions, and therefore 'free' at a symbolic level. To achieve this freedom, each one of the floor beams must span the whole width of the building, and so takes on the form of a deep lattice girder – a form usually adopted for engineering structures like bridges. A column-free floor would indeed be very useful if it was desired to install an ice hockey rink or a dodgem car fairground. So far such uses have not proved necessary for the Pompidou to fulfil its function as a library and an art gallery. So in the interest of *possibilities*, the structure has been greatly inflated, making it monumental and heroic in scale. Measured in terms of efficacy, the structure has been exaggerated and made larger than needed for normal requirements. So both structure and space, in an elegant interaction, combine to declare an ideological commitment.

This aspect of the building, although in strict terms impractical, does not arise out of any inadequacy on the part of the architects, but out of a desire to reach out to the future. It is precisely this desire which lifts the building into the realm of rhetoric and sustains the mythic aspect of its modernity. People have responded in due measure, and the building has been immensely popular, thereby no doubt justifying its expense, far beyond what strict cost accounting would have allowed. Thus, for function to exist as a myth, it has to be made larger than life and given the strangeness of things still to come. It points to a mythic future, beckons to Utopia.[15]

Moreover, when the origins of its myth are realised, it is not difficult to see the High Tech as a style. With several of its British proponents knighted, it is evident that, in Britain at least, that approach has achieved pre-eminence and is now preferred by the Establishment. Foster, Rogers, and now Hopkins, are the names, not so much of individual architects, as of the proponents of a style that can be guaranteed to deliver the goods, free from the perils of introspection, free from personal prejudice. Is it possible that the corridors of power are still running on the assumption that architecture that looks like engineering is least likely to conceal a personal vision?

Yet this preference does not work automatically. Jan Kaplicky might be quite bitter about the struggle his younger firm has had to engage in, while adopting a very similar approach, before beginning finally to achieve acceptance. Could it be that he has tempted fortune by naming his operation Future Systems? Could it be that this very name admits too much about the aspirations, common to all who strictly attempt to reveal the function, the whole function, and only the function, and at the same time to uncover the unexpected, discover a strange beauty, and deliver the future?

It is also true that this attachment to function as a source of form and a justification for strangeness is almost as old as the century, and arose not in Britain, with its attachment to Arts and Crafts, but on the Continent, where abstract ideas have always exerted an attraction. The clearest case of the dissociation of function from formal considerations must surely be the Schröder House of Gerrit Rietveld, where the architect was successful in suggesting that architecture could be brought squarely into art. Radically different from the terrace of bourgeois apartments against which it is propped, it emerges even today as an expressive gesture of the artist, proclaiming its refusal of norms and conventions. By contrast with its immediate context, it stands out as an isolated individual object, a colourful play of abstract forms: clearly, an 'artistic' statement.

What is important for us here is to take note of the way the interior was designed, not as a work of art, but as a functional mechanism. The upper floor can be enjoyed as 'free' space, by means of fold-away or sliding partitions. When the partitions are drawn out to the centre, the various functions of sleeping, bathing, eating and playing music, are differentiated and separated. In the development of the Modern style, nothing is of

Gerrit Rietveld, Schröder House, Utrecht, 1924

greater interest than the way that architecture as art was conflated with architecture as functional science. The mediating concept was that of the *machine*. The status of fine art clearly depends on its being differentiated from applied art: only something which is useless in the practical sense has the capacity to express aspirations that go beyond convenience and use. However, the machine, as concept, is imbued with mystery. It has the same dark side as the concept of a robot, as is evident from the way it was used by Duchamp and Picabia. The house as *machine à habiter* is mysterious, distanced from any idea of craft, with its connotations of decoration and established tradition.

In the Schröder House, the exterior approaches the status of a fine art object. But this detachment from practical life cannot survive the intimacy of actual use, which impinges on the interior. The interior is no longer an object of contemplation, but a convenience. The aesthetic of the exterior, apparently the result of pure feeling, has given way to a hybrid confection, part utility, part decoration. There are bright colours, abstract forms, but they are fragmented, no longer cohesive as an artistic 'statement'. There is, certainly, a strong sense of style, as well as of *de stijl*. But the totality no longer acts as a single composition acting on the spirit, it is determined by practical considerations. Everything is all too clearly representative of its use: a chair for sitting, a stove for warmth. We are living in a material world, the real world. In no sense are we inhabiting the spirit of the composition projected on the exterior. The plastic unity of the exterior returns only as fragments, as decoration. The power of the house lies in its transformational capability, its agility. It is intended to be used, it is not a work of art, but a miracle of accommodation. It seems then, that from its inception, Modern architecture has been dominated by function, more correctly, by a *myth* of function. It has taken the best part of eighty years for this myth to crumble.

Of course, there is a practical sense in which buildings must fulfil their function, must 'work'. And there is a conventional sense in which the way buildings work should indeed be attuned to the needs and attitudes of the day. We can expect them, therefore, just as clothes and cars do, to express not only the habits of the day, but the expectations of the day, that is, our feelings about future possibilities and lifestyles. Such attitudes are perfectly understandable, and it is also understandable that designers will make large claims about their latest product, in an attempt to gain a market share in its exploitation. Architecture, however, has not only conformed to the culture of the latest thing, but in doing so has claimed to be ruled by a scientific precision that cannot apply to activities governed by conventions.

The needs of the body, in all its variants of lying, sitting, standing, walking and working, are constrained by biology as well as by convention, and biological needs do not change with the speed of social conventions. It follows that many old houses are perfectly adaptable to modern living. It is changes in convention that make it necessary for us to 'modernise' them, usually in the areas pertaining to ablution and food preparation, that is, bathroom and kitchen, where we do have different expectations and technology. However, it is no longer believed that by following functional needs very closely, strange and wonderful forms will arise all by themselves. If something strange and wonderful is wanted, the architect has to invent it, just like any other artist.

This, I think, is the reason why architects have been looking back to the Russian Constructivists for inspiration, to a time when function had not yet come to dominate the Modern Movement. The Constructivists also looked to the future, but they were less inhibited in seeing it with an artist's sense of discovery, and in their vision of building they were able to assume the freedom to express feelings directly. The actual achievements in built form proved elusive – this is evident if one compares what Melnikov built to what he drew. However, within a graphic universe, gravity was not so powerful. Today, architects are trying to recover that freedom of expression, by going back to the point reached by the Constructivists in the early twenties.

Malevich's *Suprematist Architecture* of 1923 is one of the most influential images of the Modern Movement, produced by a member of the avant-garde, placing the idea of a new architecture in the framework of an avant-garde polemic. The new architecture is montaged onto a photo of New York, and so is made to represent a coming revolution, in which the New not only modifies the Old, but replaces it altogether. In Malevich's montage, New York, the first city of the New World, is made to look old. Everything was to be done again, anew, this time with the benefit of modernity, that is, with the ability to shed conventions and abstract the essentials. It conflates the advantage of

Malevich, Suprematist Architecture, 1923, montage

abstraction as a method and as a vision, as thought process and as a style. The result: architecture becomes part of a new Utopia.

If Utopia has not come about, it is not because the Russians got it wrong or that Stalin perverted the new state, it is because Utopia is by definition excluded from dialectics. It appears within dialectics only as a mirage that beckons. This is to do with the extraordinary appeal of Utopia as an idea, the way it lent itself both to political idealism and to the cult of the artist as a visionary. For a moment the artist's vision became a political weapon. Expectations of a new world were removed from the time scale of history, history as a succession of events, and placed in a context of instant success, at one with the speed of thought. The utopia represented by Malevich exists in an ideal realm, a realm that is, properly speaking Nowhere, precisely because it is an ideal.

By the use of photomontage Malevich privileges the new in a peculiar way, making it appear imminent, a part of the unfolding of events, a part of the history of the immediate future (to use Reyner Banham's phrase). There is no reason why an avant-garde polemic should not appropriate an architectural image, but this is not the same thing as re-defining the actual means of production of architecture, which remain tied to social realities that change only comparatively slowly, because they require changes in the deep structure of society itself. The confusion of these two separate things is still at large today, mixing up the idea of an avant-garde vision and the technological expectations of the immediate future.

Since the twenties our understanding of the world has become more complex and less reassuring. In the twenties the need was to grasp the future in order to relinquish the illusions of the *ancien régime*. Today, our need is to grasp a future that will protect us from uncertainty and conflict. The illusions of the *ancien régime* have long since faded, but the illusions of Modernism are evidently still necessary to us.

POSITIVE FUTURES:
RE-ANIMATING THE OLD

■ We have discussed the complexity of cultural history and the continuous process, dialectical in nature, by which culture extends itself through its response to events and by the effort of countless individuals. It follows that for every single event of history there is a corresponding multiple reflection in culture, and that within culture past history is never static but is constantly seen from a new present, and is therefore constantly under review.

The single historian can never achieve a complete understanding of any sequence of the past, still less give a complete account of it. The distant past is already clouded by loss of primary material, erosion of secondary material, re-evaluation of old facts and opinions, new questions posed too late, and hundreds of other factors which amount to a shifting framework borne on the ideology of the times. Whatever the object of study can mean to us, it is virtually impossible to know what it meant to them. Recent history is clouded by the deaths of protagonists and eye-witnesses, the coming to light of facts not known during the protagonists' lifetimes, the discovery of new material that supports a different account from the one previously accepted. Even in a small temporal difference, there are significant shifts in the ideological framework. In spite of access to eye-witnesses, the history of the very recent past is even more subject to re-evaluation, as the events are still causing repercussions that change them, before they can be painted into a consistent picture. The historian looks backward, from the rear of the train, and new events that suddenly appear in his vision are moving too fast to grasp. The distant view does not change much, but is obscured by mist. We are suspended between the desire to write and to read, a comprehensible story and the resistance that facts present to the credibility of the narrative, even when their incontrovertible status is challenged.

Among the many sources that the historian has to attend to are the physical constructions left by a former state of society. Buildings are a vital source for the cultural historian, less explicative than documents, perhaps, but in so far as they represent in their time a considerable economic investment, they present substantive evidence of contemporary values. The archaeologist pays attention to the buildings erected by exotic tribes whose culture he wants to understand; our buildings will in turn provide evidence for future archaeologists. Important buildings conceived as a form of glorification used to be built for posterity – as monuments to a ruler, to an institution, to a powerful individual. They were built to last. Today, buildings that answer to a transitory need are capable of lasting for many years: a building that can last ten years will be good for a hundred. However, our means of disposing of buildings has also progressed, and today, when a building occupies land that suddenly increases in value, it offers little resistance to the forces of change. Stone and concrete are no longer 'permanent' materials. Moreover, from the invention of photography onwards, there are more forms of documentation of the environment available, so that other records are extant. One of the most telling kinds of evidence is the film or video, combining a visual record with a sound track, and material of this kind vastly extends the range and plenitude of the archive that becomes available with every passing year. For every political event that is put on film – the appearance of the cavalcade, the surge of the crowd, the shot of the assassin – a record is also created of the mute background which inadvertently bears witness to it. And though the monument built out of stone no longer has the unique value it once had, it still occurs.

Monuments in public space have their function defined by society's need to re-create the past and keep alive traditions. The monument is mute, it speaks only within the force of society's ideology. The Cenotaph does nothing to slow the movement of the daily traffic that passes it by, but once a year it becomes the focus of a national ritual, and the traffic is momentarily displaced by common consent. In such cases, common consent indeed shows the force of the complicity between society and its dominant ideology. The importance of such factors is amply demonstrated by the way the Bolsheviks removed the monuments of Czarist Russia and the present generation has removed the monuments of Soviet realism, to demonstrate a change in the aspirations of society. Conversely, some statues of Queen Victoria have never been removed from their plinths in India, but now speak with a different voice, reinforcing the power of an independent India that had no need to erase them from memory, and has absorbed the relics of colonialism to its own ends. The Viceroy's House simply becomes the President's Palace.

The complicity that preserves a public meaning is a scandal to the radical critic of society and to every attempt to erase old values and substitute new ones. As a Marxist, Roland Barthes strove to unmask this complicity, half-unthinking, half-cynical, in what he saw as the false consciousness of the bourgeois society of his time. Whether it belongs to a nationalist fervour to rouse emotions or a capitalist desire to anaesthesise them, it seems to depend on a coarse approximation to togetherness, rather than leading to the fine perceptions that can be expressed

The Tomb of the Unknown Warrior and The Eternal Flame, Brussels

by an individual. Yet, by their very numbness, such symbols are not without power.

On a wet Sunday morning in Brussels, the Tomb of the Unknown Warrior seemed to represent only a distant and alien condition, irrelevant and anti-modern. Lions, heraldic devices, female muses, all speak a dead language, barely to be interpreted as part of a living tradition. But something works against its easy dismissal: in front of the Tomb, the Eternal Flame burns still – no doubt by courtesy of the Gas Company, but still it fascinates. It brings animation, and hence a kind of life, to the hoary symbols of patriotism. Because it is a living flame – like the Olympic flame in its moment of truth – it is more 'real' than the stone monument, and its presence declares an intention of society that gives one pause. Its moment will return, the ceremony will be conducted anew, and if you were affected by the history it witnesses, still more if you lost a loved one in the events it commemorates, your emotions will again be touched. In this way, a rhetorical figure unites a reality with a myth, and a dialectic is set in motion: on the one hand, the myth is re-animated, on the other, the reality is in a certain sense emptied out.

The Cenotaph and the Eternal Flame are monuments that represent an important case. Whatever one's degree of complicity or alienation in connecting to the sentiment they express, that sentiment is clearly essential to the continuation of a national identity. The flame fascinates because it is 'real', in spite of the fact that it testifies to a concealed gas supply. We know this, but we cannot ignore the social intention it represents, the will to re-animate the myth. So, even if we were passing in our camper in the early hours of a damp morning, with not a soul in sight, we would hesitate before using the flame to fry our breakfast eggs. In the same way, for the Algerian demonstrators who extinguished the Eternal Flame at the Arc de Triomphe in Paris, by a direct method only available to the men, this was for them no easy gesture, but a meaningful desecration and a courageous sign of refusal. The symbol, even if visibly an artifice, attaches itself to the political reality and remains potent. The very existence of national rituals is a testament to the continuity between past and present, and demonstrates that in spite of technology's power to change values, it encounters a resistance to complete change. At a global scale, technology leads to homogenisation and it seems that only national beliefs have the power to resist it.

Such examples help to demonstrate that, as Barthes claimed, Myth is still alive, even if it is sustained by ideology. Along with the myth of the future, there is also the myth of the past. In some ideal sense both are false and both are powerful.

The steps by which the radical artist frees himself from convention and does something shocking, are as much instigated by the need to react from the present as by divine discontent. To begin the resistance, we have to seize on a point of present pain, to re-sort aspects of the culture that have until now been held apart. From this follows the importance of provenance, of the precise point from which the artist sets out. The state of *tabula rasa* is an illusion. From this point of view it is possible to think of culture, not as clutter, from which the progressive architect has to free himself,[16] but as a field rich in possibilities, an archive that is full of ideas that can be shaken up and become the catalyst for the New.[17] The archive can be reanimated, potentially it is already *The Animated Archive*.[18] Many artists find inspiration in a master whom they seek first to equal and then to surpass. The work of thinkers and artists progresses as much by re-inventing the past as by inventing the future.

There is no question that when one is confronted by a new stone building in a Cambridge College in the Palladian style, bright as a new pin, evidently just completed, the first sensation is one of shock. This is the unexpected, all right. Is it also the New? The architect Quinlan Terry is not interested in reviving a Palladian feel, he has gone all out to re-animate a Palladian style. We may go on to criticise the Order he uses as lacking in authenticity, the capitals too small, not what Palladio would have done, and so on; such criticism merely reinforces

Quinlan Terry, Maitland Robinson Library, Downing College, Cambridge

the fact that the architect is working *in* the style, not simulating Palladio's personal signature. He will claim, and he does, that it is the Classical style that provides the framework and that it will follow that, in spite of the canon being fixed, its interpretation is open. The Classical is capable of further evolution through the twentieth century and beyond. This is perhaps not within the scope of one architect to achieve, but others may contribute, since the basis of the approach is plain and anyone may adopt it. It is open to speculation whether architects such as Robert Adam, John Simpson and Demetri Porphyrios are together forging some kind of late twentieth-century Classicism in England. It helps Terry that he appears genuinely to believe that the Classical Orders are God-given, and this brings a degree of conviction to his work that makes it very different from the Post-Modernism of, say, Robert Venturi, who thinks of himself as essentially a Modern architect, working in slippery times, working far from a fixed canon.[19]

Classical architecture lost its pre-eminence during the nineteenth century, when other possibilities began to make their appeal. However, it continued, if spasmodically, into the twentieth century. In Sweden, Sigurd Lewerentz completed his Resurrection Chapel at Enskede Cemetery in Stockholm only in 1923 – it mixes Classical motives with picturesque composition in an arresting and original way; and Gunnar Asplund continued to use the orders for family tombs through the twenties – his vault for the Rettig family constructed in 1928 makes an original but correct use of a Tuscan Doric, contemporary with his more famous Library for Stockholm, designed in a more abbreviated Neoclassical style. In the hands of these masters, Classicism co-existed with their experiments in the new non-style of Modernism.

In England, Classicism continued into the period after World War II in the work of such respected architects as Oliver Hill, Louis de Soissons, Brandon Jones and Reginald Blomfield; while an important work – Kingswalden, Bury – by an acknowledged master of Classicism (and Terry's teacher) Raymond Erith, was completed only in 1970, thus reaching into the decade of the oil crisis and the debate about Post-Modernism. Note that I have made no mention of the use, rather, the exploitation of the Classical, by the authoritarian régimes of the thirties. It is obvious that Classicism is fundamentally marked with the idea of authority, from its pagan origins, from the moment of its adoption in the Italian Renaissance as a resource of Christianity. This does not make it automatically Fascist. In any case, a very similar Classical architecture continued in the United States up to World War II as the preferred style for official buildings like post offices.

Attempts have been made to argue that Classicism is not a style, but simply the result of applying rational procedures to custom and habit.[20] It will then be the most readily identified of all the Western traditions in building, the easiest for the layman to understand, one that can adapt to many usages and still retain its identity, effectively therefore a timeless way of building. The symmetry of the building is a reflection of the symmetry of the body, and symmetry of the organism has been shown to be an advantage in the struggle for survival. Symmetry as a principle of organisation, according to Leon Krier, allows each building to establish an identity at the human scale. Following the initiative of Lewerentz, Classical ideas can be recombined in a free style, and the Classical can also be identified in a loose and relaxed vernacular. Contemporary rationalists, of whom Aldo Rossi must be the most well-known, and Giorgio Grassi the most obdurate, adopt a reduced and attenuated Classicism in preference to expressionism of any kind, as a means of keeping architecture from being possessed by individual excess, with the aim of allowing it to continue to function in the public realm, a virtue under Marxism. This approach also has the advantage of allowing construction that is both rational and cheap, as demonstrated by Rossi in the Modena Cemetery. Indeed, Rossi's perception that even in cheap buildings symmetry can be effective as a mode of composition reaches back to Palladio's discovery that simple farm buildings can be used to extend the composition of a modest house towards a useful grandeur.

However, despite these propositions, it seems that Classicism is *above all* a style, in the sense that it is based upon an explicit canon – the use of the Orders, explicitly or implicitly – along with the principle of symmetry. This style may yet be capable of extension in the future, but if it is extended merely by forming hybrids, in the manner of Post-Modernism, it will eventually lose its identity. That it has, indeed, changed enormously over the centuries since it was first codified by the Ancient Greeks is, in a way, proof that it can take many forms and express many emotions, and float upon many stages of culture, without losing its essential character. But the shock that it produces when it insists on this continuity, as in the hands of Quinlan Terry, is a shock that above all expresses the Now, the surprising survival right up to this moment of something that had been considered lost. This is possible precisely because each moment in time presents a different viewpoint.

In a way we are confronted here with a return of the old opposition between ancient and modern. The ancient idealises the past just as the modern idealises the future. The ancient accepts its place in a tradition which limits its freedom, but where it can still accommodate a challenge to renew itself by exceeding this tradition, providing it is done in good faith. The modern refuses tradition, refuses even to be considered a style, claims that it is only a regular method of work concentrating on use and function, which if faithfully executed can bring future reality into existence. It conforms to the case made for it by John Summerson when he argued that the theory of Modern architecture is based on the programme, that is on empirical reality rather than on fixed principles.

There is a certain symmetry in these positions. The one tries to make an expected outcome appear fresh. The other tries to make the unexpected come about by a natural process. In both cases a complex cultural situation is reduced to a formula. Each harbours contradictions that arise out of simplifying the present, the complex of economic and cultural factors that determine the present state of society.

In Regent's Park, along the Outer Circle just opposite the American Residency, Quinlan Terry has erected three villas conforming to a single type. They are all built in stone, in a Palladian style, all the same size, all having a central pedimental group with one bay either side, but varied in treatment to give each house an individual appeal: one is straight Palladian, one Gothick, and so on. The wrought-iron gates bear their names: Ionic Villa, Veneto Villa and Gothick Villa. They are part of a commercial development of a prime site on Crown land for leasing to the wealthy. The sale of the leaseholds is promoted

Quinlan Terry, Villas in Regent's Park, London

by a plush brochure, and it is clear that the operation is essentially the same as for the sort of variegated plot development on suburban estates, where you can choose between Ranch, Colonial, Tudor and so on, except that it is about as far up-market as is possible. Only the very affluent can afford this privilege of preference.

Coming upon this group of villas in Regent's Park could not convey anything more different from the unique encounters one makes in Maser or in Fratta Polesine in the Veneto, where each house speaks of a complete way of life. Palladio too was successful in anticipating the needs of his clients, particularly their desire to become landowners and acquire country estates in a period of economic upheaval, as the conditions of trade altered and the Republic of Venice began its fatal descent from being the world trade centre of its time. Those were times of change too, but both Palladio and his clients still shared the belief in the God-given status of the Orders. The built reality in Regent's Park is impressed with a very different social order, and it makes clear that the Classical style has survived here only by entering the commercial framework that makes *Nostalgia* and *Futuristic* equally accessible as clichés, that is by courting the market. With the loss of shared belief, something vital has disappeared from the situation. In this case it is possible to accept that the architect himself works from conviction, but the scene he makes betrays a very different set of convictions. Once again, architecture pays the price for being embedded in a social situation, not even apparently free.

THE LOSS OF THE ABSOLUTE

■ Loss of belief in the Classical Orders is only one symptom of the changes in our world that have followed upon the success of material science. Since the Copernican revolution, causal explanation has offered more convincing explanations than the morally inspired hierarchies offered by organised religion. Where it was once believed that not a sparrow could fall to the ground without God's supervision, we now understand that God is otherwise occupied. Voltaire had to make a close argument to show that the Lisbon earthquake was not retribution for sin, but a combination of chance and nature. Today, ordinary people, in the West at least, have begun to understand that chance and the statistics of chance account for many things that were formerly thought to be part of a Divine Intention. The loss of a jealous God is for many of us a liberation, but liberty is bought at a price, and the price in this case is a loss of the rule system that used to support the sense of personal responsibility. Nothing used to happen without being intended, whether by God or Man, and God was a way of writing a sort of human agency into the sky. Everything was impregnated with meaning and all events were linked to a human scale of values, involving our compliance or resistance, and so our feelings, whether jubilation, reward, guilt or remorse.

Today, the guilt has migrated to other regions, to those aspects of God that can be represented by our parents and teachers, and by the memories of their precepts that have entered our subconscious. If we wake up at night in momentary terror, it is more to do with the unwinding of unconscious memories than with our sense of sin. As the concept of sin has weakened, the concept of blame has been strengthened. If we are unhappy now, we must have been ill-treated, perhaps abused. Where can the blame be laid now? It is hard to endure tribulations for which there is nobody to blame. To a large extent we still see the world in terms of the nursery, complaining when some chance outcome strikes us as being most unfair. A more or less human agency must be involved. Forest fires, formerly thought to be part of the divine process of retribution, are now invariably attributed to incendiarism. The absence of divine providence is betrayed in the eagerness to sue: after the earthquake, *somebody* must have been at fault.

As the secular explanation of how things happen becomes dominant, we are still anxious to read intentions into our surroundings, just as on summer evenings with our children we used to play at seeing faces in the clouds. The world we see is deeply ambiguous, and so too are our responses. Willing to see chance as unprejudiced – somebody has to win the jackpot, it could just as well be me – we also people the world with deities like good luck and winning combinations, or malign forces like vicious neighbours and corrupt politicians, believing the worst of other people and other races. Conversely, where murder used to be primarily a family event, it is increasingly the result of chance, such as gratuitous shots from a passing car. Thieves and robbers increasingly pick on defenceless people, just as the beast of prey singles out the wounded animal. In a secular universe, retribution recedes and moral responsibility fades.

Philosophy is still struggling with the problem of how to sustain values in a valueless world. If truth itself is elusive, as modern philosophy suggests, what happens to the clearcut division of right and wrong? If our smallest actions are no longer subject to divine supervision, what happens to the concept of sin, and of moral responsibility? Are guilt and remorse necessary for good behaviour, or unnecessary barriers to enjoyment? Is respect only assured by superior force? If perceptions of pleasure are available for the price of a pill, what use is imagination? Such questions are no longer treated as answerable. The attitudes they expressed have been displaced into a world system, which, like the Internet, is both mechanical and predictable, and full of opportunities, but also unpredictable in places, full of strange dangers and faceless robbers, viruses and black holes. As we learn from playing computer games, at any moment we may be zapped.

This framework of accident replaces the moral universe, and this in turn is a probable explanation of our need to overcompensate in ideological terms. Ideologies are not universal systems of belief, but consolatory treaties between those who share aspirations. Our ideologies work only for us, or only for part of the time. The world is now ruptured into those who share our ideas and those for whom they do not even exist. It is not unexpected then that excessive worship of the past or of the future become two of the ways in which some structure can be reconstructed and some certainty be regained.

The awareness of history as a progression, where superior knowledge ousts inferior knowledge, produces two opposing views, broadly, the forward and the backward view. Either we are advancing towards total knowledge or we are retreating from a condition of redemption to a condition of damnation. Even in the Christian system there was always the idea of history coming to an end with the division of the world into sheep and goats. The modern secular system has taken over this aspect of ancient eschatology, giving it a basis in physical science, but keeping a certain morality to the extent that the biosphere is perceived not as a robust birthright but as a fragile balance.

It is this attitude which lurks in the Green movement, which looks to the future not exactly as a time of fulfilment and splendid enjoyment, but as a time when problems come home to roost at a global scale. If we can detect the sense of sin to some degree reincarnated in this movement, this is not to deny its force. Rational prediction of the future has to include the case where our own actions have induced an unexpected and unwelcome outcome. With the total power of the hydrogen bombs now at our disposal, we have achieved the ability to blow the biosphere away, should we be mad enough to do so; and if this seems unlikely, it is sobering to remember that for the individual who feels thwarted and outcast, suicide can exert an enormous attraction, as when Samson decided to pull down the alien temple which held him prisoner.

There is still hope that if enough people share a rational basis, this outcome will be avoided. In the case of the loss of the ozone layer, there is hope that governments will finally be able to control emissions sufficiently to reverse the phenomenon. In the case of global warming, there is hope that conditions will change slowly enough to be brought progressively under control. In the case of excess population and limited food production, there is hope that science will be able to open the way for new technological miracles, by growing food in the seas, or on space stations, or establishing colonies on the moon. Such possibilities are not necessarily fantastic, but we have made little progress in understanding the way in which human behaviour will have to accommodate such outcomes, if they prove necessary. That will be for somebody else to worry about. On the whole, our attitude remains optimistic.

Rational predictions of future problems have had little effect on present levels of consumption. Change is welcomed if it appears to profit us, rejected if it reduces our profits. When I talk to right-wing economists about global warming, they discount it as nothing but leftist propaganda, and declare that the facts in themselves are ambiguous, meaning that there is not as yet sufficient reason to disturb the market. This response is evidently an indication that raising doubts about the wisdom of continuing to exploit the environment is itself dangerous thinking; merely to express these doubts could be enough to undermine confidence and disturb the continuity of the market. Even when we are disposed to believe in negative futures that might result from global warming, or ozone depletion or loss of species or destruction of the rain forests, we are still disposed to believe that science will rescue us in good time.

The very enjoyment we experience in negative futures and the possibility of social breakdown (as depicted in the films *Blade Runner* or *Mad Max*) shows that we are as comfortable with these fantasies as with old horror stories like *Frankenstein*. Their existence, as fiction, confirms them as a new genre of ghost stories, meant to frighten us without making us seriously afraid. We do not believe in ghosts any more, except as an occasion for fun, as in the movie *Ghostbusters*. We are pretty sure that the future is going to be a positive one. And I am sure that there is a sense in which everyone believes, and wants to believe, that progress is inevitable.

In retrospect, this optimism has lasted for most of the twentieth century. Given that the perfectibility of man was an Enlightenment invention and became the basis for Hegel's vision of a world that would prove to be as much the creation of logic as was mathematics, this vision has gradually migrated from a logical to a technological level. Certainly it lies behind the hope that, with function as a basis, all architectural problems could be solved. It is written into the myth of modernity. It also sustained the euphoria of the Italian Futurists and the Russian Constructivists. In these cases, however, the technological element was weak: both were overtaken by political restructuring and the technological future was discovered only within the freer discourse of the democracies. Francis Fukuyama's optimistic account of the End of History [21] assumes that only within the structure of liberal democracy can freedom of thought be extended, unbroken, to assure the conditions under which scientific discovery can occur. This, too, we would like to believe, in spite of ominous indications that pure science is becoming increasingly subject to Governmental control in order to assure its resource base.[22]

There is therefore an ironic aspect in the way that architecture has recently returned to the future, and to a futurism of a more technological slant; but it has also returned, after an interval of some three-quarters of a century, to the promise of abstraction and the freedom of gesture that it confers. In the twenties it was this freedom that the Russian Constructivists assumed. In the aftermath of the Russian Revolution, as servants of a new society in the making, they claimed exactly the same freedom of action as the radical artists. The economic situation of the nascent Soviet Union did not allow a ready deployment of this artistic talent into the practical problems of the industrialisation of the building industry. Only Melnikov managed to build something and his built projects are disappointing in comparison to the ones that never got beyond the drawing board. In any case, this freedom potentially conferred by the use of abstract forms was decisively rejected by the great majority of the architects of the heroic period in favour of a disciplined rationalism, modelled on the behaviour of the scientist rather than the artist. Today there is a new willingness to see architecture as a form of art, governed by function, certainly, but not entirely determined by it. This transition has been aided by the development of computer graphics and the blurring of the distinction between drawing as information and drawing as emotion.

Rem Koolhaas and Zaha Hadid are two architects, both of whom formerly worked together in the Office of Metropolitan Architecture, who have used graphic presentation to effect a *rapprochement* between the drawing as information and the drawing as emotion. In such presentations, the building appears to float in an abstract universe, weightless, ideal. But this is no longer a quality that is proper only to the drawing, as it was with Malevich or El Lissitzky. It is now assumed that technology

LEFT: Rem Koolhaas, project for apartment building, Rotterdam;
RIGHT: Zaha Hadid, planetary architecture

will be successful in re-creating the drawing as built reality, without loss of the emotion. Thus the chasm that separated Melnikov's fantastic drawings from the banality of his constructions is effectively cancelled by the power of technology to implement fantasy. If technology can create virtual reality, it can create an equivalent reality. Architecture can now envisage a functionality that is not simply rational, or conceived in a Cartesian mode, but which occupies an artistic shell like a kind of concierge, a functionary rather than a controlling spirit. The spirit is now, again, independent of the external constraints, even if it must take account of them. Technology, instead of providing the source of the form and the meaning, acts to reconcile the artist's vision with the causal world.

It is true that with Koolhaas this approach is not devoid of an ironic and potentially tragic dimension. In delivering us over to a technological universe, he somehow makes us aware as much of loss as of gain. The emotion is exaggerated beyond what the information will bear, so that the reality of his world enters the surreal. Rejecting the sense of repletion that the smooth technological interior projects, he allows harsh notes and unexpected intrusions to appear, insisting on the play of chance. The finished surface does not blend together different materials but allows their junctions to clash or appear improvisatory. He recapitulates many of the prismatic forms of early modern buildings but his awareness of them as precedent makes *us* aware of them too and draws our attention to important differences that make our cultural envelope already very different from that of the twenties and thirties. His buildings are disturbing rather than reassuring, and in this he opens us up to the loss of the very values to which the buildings of the heroic period seemed to testify. His Modernism is not an unconscious continuation of modernity but a narcissistic questioning of it. It seems to say, this is modern life: is this what we want? By his reiteration of modernist forms Koolhaas increases our angst, somehow suggesting that these forms have already suffered an irretrievable loss of meaning.

Peter Eisenman is an architect who has made his reputation by aggressively facing up to the loss of absolute values. It is the philosophical question which is his point of departure. In the context of this discussion, he is of interest precisely because he has never seized on the technological future as a 'solution'. It is true that the conditions of practice in the United States do not favour an ideological exaggeration of space and structure, as they have done in Europe. America has always worked on the primacy of *image* as the key element in motivation, and therefore in change. Automobiles, for example, must look futuristic before being dangerously innovative, and buildings should look daring rather than being dangerously expensive to construct. The absence of an American branch of the High Tech style is significant. Eisenman is refreshing because he does not look to a future that will solve practical problems and at the same time discover a new poetics out of the functional conditions. He uses the technology available to construct enigmas that throw into doubt the very concept of meaning.

In his design for the Convention Center at Columbus, Eisenman throws together two sets of forms that suggest two very different things: the large halls, whose volumes create ribbons of space and whose roofs create twisted decks reminiscent of a freeway intersection; and the smaller units of wall in which these ribbons terminate, forming a kind of street facade.

Peter Eisenman, Convention Center, Columbus, Ohio

Nothing here is exactly what it seems. The tangle of halls in fact provides the unitary space the convention requires and the row of walls provides the site for the pre-convention publicity. At the metaphoric level, the building as a whole expresses a clash between the scale of the automobile city and the scale of the old city street. The apparently separate terminations of the ribbons of space along a common frontage mock the convention of the historic city, whereby separate acts of building formerly joined together to express the social unity of the gridded plan. Thus, if the building conforms to its functional requirements, it does not draw its poetic from them. It is, rather, an example of the way that in recent years, abstraction and expression have been drawn together in order to reassert the architect's right to propose form out of his own introspection, instead of from an unadulterated analysis of the requirements.

At the same time the design is, as much as anything, an embodiment of the argument about *abstraction* and *representation* that Eisenman and his former colleague, Michael Graves, have been engaged in for years; but this is only to suggest the conditions of its genesis. Both architects belonged to the group known as *The New York Five*, and the formation of that group helped them to adopt new attitudes that, individually, they might not have been able to define. Collectively, the group was representative of a new generation that wanted to restate the terms on which European Modernism could be followed in the very different conditions of an American time and place. Instead of the restricted horizon of European revolution, in revolt against the stifling restrictions of the *ancien régime*, they have to deal with the looser conditions induced by a managerial revolution, and at the same time confront the wider horizon of an immense country where the space must be occupied and where the wilderness itself provides a witness to the insecurity of the universe. The special conditions of the United States were set by the strange coincidence of mass production and an expanding land frontier. The first successful factory for assembling pieces according to a principle of a defined dimensional tolerance (the Winchester Rifle) introduced an expanding economic framework at the very moment when the country was being drawn together by the new railroads. The vertiginous growth of cities like Chicago is not to be found anywhere else, until perhaps we arrive at the China of the 1990s.

The insecurity of life can be expressed in many kinds of buildings. As early as 1971, the Japanese architect Monta Mozuma pioneered the mixing of conceptualism and expressionism with his *Anti-Dwelling Box*. It takes the dwelling out of ordinary life and makes of it a kind of theatre of the absurd. The Japanese have been adept at imitating many trends in Western technology, including the space and structure of modern architecture. However, everything they have taken, they have transmuted in placing it within their own culture. One suspects that their attitude towards ritual, according it equal power when observed socially and when observed by a single individual, has allowed them to place ritual space more firmly into the singular architectural setting. As a result, a simple object, such as a private house, can become the vehicle for the expression of a questioning of the function of a house. If this house provides shelter and comfort, it draws its poetic from a questioning of these very concepts.

Mozuma's *Anti-Dwelling Box* pre-dates by some fifteen years a rather similar experiment by the Californian architect Thom

LEFT: Monta Mozuma, Anti-Dwelling Box, 1972; RIGHT: Thom Mayne, Orrery for Kate Mantilini, 1987

Mayne in 1987. His Orrery for Kate Mantilini is really a machine for rendering poetic the way light falls into a complex space. It can also function as a house, but not by following the convention for a house. It seems that in working for a personal client who is basically sympathetic to the idea of the poetics of space, the architect can hope to escape from the impersonal pressures of professionalism and the suffocation of normative values, thereby exploring a range of new sensations and the disturbing side of life.

Given the range of situations for Modern buildings, there are many opportunities for the architect to satisfy artistic fantasy without denying function. At the Braun Pharmaceutical Factory in Melsungen, Stirling was able to do this and leave a satisfied client. Georg Braun had even invited Stirling to build a factory that would be perceived as 'artistic', as a masterpiece of architecture, even if it cost just a little more (it was three per cent more, he decided).[23] This factory by Stirling-Wilford, with the collaboration of Walter Nägeli, is indeed an extraordinary building, radical in its reinterpretation of forms that were originally invented by the masters of the Modern Movement. There are surreal moments here, as there are in the buildings of Rem Koolhaas. It is like Modern architecture taken into meditation. Forms that were once the expression of a considered rationality are now expressive of an ambiguous inner life.

Stirling-Wilford with Walter Nägeli, Braun Factory, Melsungen

This was possible because it was in a rural site, remote from the city, even from the town of Melsungen. The duty towards representation becomes problematic for the modern architect only when he is called to build in the city, with all its accumulated conventions and its essentially social space. The building in the city cannot be an entire world to itself, standing out against nature, but is already framed in a setting that, although at any one time apparently stable, is all the time in motion. In this respect, the city, viewed as a meaningful structure that accepts individual utterances, bears a strange resemblance to language, which is perfectly fixed for us at the time we use it, but is found later on to have been all the time in evolution. To survive in that setting, the architect must very firmly review the framework in which he acts, the inescapable demands of the common measure, and the incidence of change, which more easily accepts increments than it can be bent to total design. We might say that he must launch his building into a moving stream, and learn the wisdom of uncertainty.

THE WISDOM OF UNCERTAINTY

■ The loss of absolute values does not imply the end of the world. In so far as the belief in absolute values was only possible because of particular beliefs that formed part of the religious *credo*, it went beyond the credible and formed a constraining system that in the end amounted to a web of superstitious fear. Fear of eternal damnation can be interpreted in terms of physical torture, or of having been recorded in some final statement of accounts as having made the wrong choice. Fear does not seem the best basis for being good.

To lose that entanglement may prove to be liberating, although it challenges us to define the ethical in a philosophical rather than a religious way. It is probably easier for someone like myself to express such a hope, in personal reaction to a Calvinistic upbringing which seemed to advocate good behaviour merely as a recipe to escape punishment, rather than as an end worthy in itself. To be able to pursue an ethical way of life without the threat of eternal punishment might not only be liberating, but also consolatory in an entirely different way. That, I suppose, is the voice of the liberal, perhaps of the Liberal Democrat. If absolute values went with the era of absolute monarchy, we clearly need to create a system of values suitable for the kind of organisation that we call a modern democracy. This could even be re-stated as the essential project of modernity. Except that we cannot forget that mankind has been capable of great evil, whether or not in the name of religious belief, and continues to be capable of great evil. The twentieth century has been as full of evil as any other. Drugs and crime, cruelty and indifference, war and murder, alas, are all part of our total way of life.

Although the *credo* is an essential part of any culture, it is possible to view it as *less* than the culture, and, to the extent that it attempts to erect a verbal system as its representation, is itself impregnated with the *logos* and with ideology. Seen in this way, it is only a part of a culture which in turn is a total way of life. The religious aspects of a culture are stronger as part of that way of life – for example, as a guide to behaviour – than they are once formulated as a belief and erected as a system alongside it.

I have suggested that natural language exceeds any set of propositions that can be formulated within it. The difficulty of acquiring a natural language without living with those who speak it emphasises that not all that it means can be adequately reflected in the grammar and the dictionary, essential as these are for acquiring a working knowledge of it. Noam Chomsky's difficulty in teaching a machine to spontaneously generate meaningful sentences in English suggests the same thing. But natural language is an artefact we have constructed, or rather, evolved. We have made it, but we cannot exactly explain how, or reduce it to formulae. It does not seem unduly pessimistic to point to the level of complexity that we have achieved with natural language, and see this complexity as intimately bound up with the structure of the human brain – including what we may surmise about the subconscious – and with the complexity of the mind, and of the cultural envelope within which our way of life finds expression. It is true that with the scientific method we have begun to unravel the complexity of nature, but the closer this investigation comes to the forms of life, the less thorough and the more tentative it seems to be.

The community does not yet agree as to whether the perfection of a robot that can speak perfect English and write good poems will demonstrate a vital difference between us and our artefacts, or pronounce whether or not such an achievement will be a good thing for the future of the human race. In Western culture, the robot that takes over and coldly replaces us because of our logical deficiencies is one of the nightmares that we frighten ourselves with.

It is salutary, I believe, to make this distinction between the complexity of the artefacts we have evolved and the models we have constructed. As expressions of our culture, language is probably the most essential. All cultures have possessed a natural language. It is then interesting to turn to our physical environment and ask about the genesis of the city. Not all cultures have had cities, but no powerful cultures have not. The city may be thought of as an artefact we have constructed; it may also be thought of as an artefact we have evolved. Like language, we have created it over time. We can exist without it but we have not been able to extend our culture without city life. And now we do not exactly know what to do about it, because it has reached a level of complexity and intricacy that is not adequately reflected in our analysis of it. Is it not, like our language, an expression of our culture that reaches beyond the level of voluntary action?

The sense of the city being an essential part of our culture is reinforced when we consider what we do when it is taken away from us. The Poles reconstructed a large tract of old Warsaw when it was obliterated in the War, for it had become an essential aspect of their national identity. The French did much the same with Caen. The young United States built Washington in order to retain the symbols of majesty that had been codified within the Classical architecture of Europe – dome, pediment and colonnade – and make them the expressions of the sovereignty of the people under freedom. In the new Berlin, the Friedrichstrasse is a total building site, an essential project to express the capitalism (hopefully, a democratic capitalism) that offers it a new future. The different way in which major projects are currently being undertaken in Paris and London is a perfect expression of the approach each country has to questions of grandeur and public accessibility. At the same time, no planned city has entered real life without evolving beyond the reduced model of its originating structure. Welwyn and Letchworth are now real places in a way that has not quite been achieved as yet by Stevenage and Milton Keynes. We might spare a thought for the future of Esperanto – the designed language that was expected to be a *lingua franca* for all the nations and further international understanding. It never got beyond the design stage and into the process of evolution.

One can regret the opportunity that London lost when the City Fathers rejected Wren's Reconstruction Plan after the Great Fire; one can regret that Wren had to modify his plan for St Paul's at the behest of the Church in order to preserve the medieval plan; one can regret that the Houses of Parliament were dressed in a Perpendicular style at odds with their classical layout. Such prejudices in favour of the medieval are themselves part of English culture and can be interpreted as obstinacy or endearing conservatism according to point of view.

The way in which the city, as concept, exceeds the capability of the individual building, has not yet been properly appreciated. Le Corbusier very neatly extended one building into a design for a city – the city of two million – simply by replicating it on a square grid. We can be glad that the Voisin plan was not imposed on Paris, a fate which would have been worse than extensive war damage. Architects, on the whole, have been the last ones to see that more than one contiguous building by the same hand does not easily enter into the pattern of evolution on which the continued vitality of the city depends.

Natalie DeBlois (for SOM), Pepsi-Cola Building, New York, street view and street front

*LEFT: Advertisement for energy-efficient design: vacuum flask as building;.
RIGHT: Alvaro Siza, Borges & Irmao Bank, Lisbon*

Yet, even in the city, the architect can negotiate a certain freedom. It may not be necessary to repeat the forms of the buildings on either side, which would only result in a terrible sameness. Sometimes it is enough to observe some aspects of scale, or just size. One of my favourite modern buildings in New York City is the Pepsi-Cola Building in Park Avenue by Natalie DeBlois, in the office of SOM. It is good-looking, and a thoroughly modern miss, superbly ignoring the predominantly brick architecture of Park Avenue. But it does conform to the height restrictions which make this street so effective, and in this way it conforms, yet preserves a vital freshness.

In an advertisement printed by the Electricity Council of Britain to promote energy-efficient building, a vacuum flask is substituted for a building in a high street. It does look odd but it also puts across a point. Would it be so offensive if it were in fact built? It conforms in height and plot width to the buildings in context, if you omit the teapot on top. It is set in a little commercial street of mixed character, not a street of national heritage. Perhaps it is over the top, but in this kind of setting it is almost all right, because it lies right at a boundary between two worlds.

Alvaro Siza's Bank is, in one sense, an intrusion into the street, but not so abrupt as to destroy its continuity. Rather, it creates a welcome variety. Where building in the city is concerned,

LEFT: Alvaro Siza, Corner Building, Kreuzberg, Berlin, 1980;
RIGHT: Crabtree et al, Peter Jones, Sloane Square, London

the context sets limits, not only of dimension, but of meaning. Yet this need not lead to a deadening conformity. It seems to me that there is quite a space in which to find a way to dramatise the new without completely disrupting the old.

New buildings can actually take their unusual shape from their context, so dramatising the shape of the street itself. Alvaro Siza's Corner Building in the Kreuzberg area of Berlin exploits its situation in an unexpected way without destroying the shape of the street, indeed it enhances it. It is reminiscent of the way Crabtree's department store, Peter Jones, in Sloane Square, London, enhances the shape of the square and articulates its relation to King's Road. This building has long been accepted by Londoners as a well-loved part of the scenery, the fate that awaits even good buildings that in time become an integral part of the city.

Even Gehry, who loves to *épater* the bourgeoisie in the States, was sensitive towards the design of the building in Paris, in the heart of la France Légère. His American Centre at Bercy respects the boulevard, while breaking down into a light-hearted play of forms on the side towards the park. Of course, the building in this kind of case accepts its representational duty, does not expect to make an entirely radical statement about the horizon of expression, or the end of civilisation. Gehry has been criticised by some for not being radical here. In a case

Frank Gehry, American Centre, Paris, 1994, side to boulevard and side to park

which highlights again the difference between the American and European context, the architect made a careful decision about the degree of respect and the degree of freedom he deemed appropriate.

There is an interesting aspect, it seems to me, about the Centre Beaubourg by Piano and Rogers. It was meant to be a pretty radical statement, indeed a banner of the High Tech approach, in favour of siding with the future and rejecting convention. Yet, in its situation in Paris, its rectangular footprint confirms the shape of the Rue de Renard on one side, while forming a perfectly acceptable city square on the other.

Indeed, if we look more closely at the form of the Place Pompidou, it is not only in itself rectangular, but shelves down to the entrance. Does this not remind us of another famous public square which shelves down to the mayor's office? The Campo in Siena seems to lurk behind the Place Pompidou, and after all, both Piano and Rogers would have been utterly familiar with it as a model. The connection is confirmed, perhaps, by the way that Sir Richard, in his *Reith Lectures*, came out strongly in favour of the dense European city. Its problems – congestion, pollution, contingency – are in his view to be solved by the application of science. It is worth pointing out that whereas the city has no problem in absorbing his Lloyd's Building as a unique character in the city, it might not survive

LEFT: Place Pompidou, Paris; RIGHT: The Campo, Siena

his proposals to transform a whole stretch of the north bank of the Thames by turning it into a linked series of towers and bridges in the High Tech manner, thus creating a homogenous and highly indigestible chunk of real estate.

Modern architecture wanted to be a part of the future, but after three-quarters of a century, the future it anticipated is not quite the future we got. Now, the Modern Movement has its own history, replete with Jencksian categories like Post-Modern, Late-Modern, and so on. We begin to disbelieve the apocalyptic note of its founders, which looked to everything becoming more different that it turned out. We have the same note sounded today by the deconstructionists who want us to believe that society is in a metaphysical crisis, and can only be saved – it is the traditional message of the evangelist – by conformity to a new creed. Society, it is true, is in a crisis. It is a crisis that has more to do with ecological disaster and racial mayhem than with choosing the right style in art. In this sense, the more modern life comes to depend on human management, the more dangerous become our mistakes.

However, within architecture it is absurd to hope to express the nature of our problems in artistic form, in order to feel that we have confronted the worst and know it and accept it in advance. This is not the way to manage the future; in fact, it rather contributes to a form of hysteria.

It may be salutary, rather, to recognise the *continuity* in the forms of modern architecture, even in what purports to be the most radical modern architecture. In this connection I'd like to advance the case of Foster's Sainsbury Centre. It is built in the form of an industrial shed, and it was considered a radical approach to propose an industrial form for an art gallery in the heart of a rural campus, at the University of East Anglia. However, the industrial shed has a long pedigree, going back through such obvious examples as Peter Behrens' AEG Turbine Shed, through Ferdinand Dutert's Galerie des Machines to . . . well, maybe to King's College Chapel, a noble shed, but one that conforms impeccably to the formal description of a shed as a series of identical structural bays proceeding inexorably from one end to the other. In this light, the Sainsbury Centre would be placed in a perspective of more than three centuries.

However, there is a more exact sense in which the Sainsbury Centre develops some central themes of modernity, and thereby shows its debt to the evolution of the Modern style. It follows the convention whereby the side walls act as a container, concentrating space into a linear sequence, and strongly differentiating the sides from the ends, which are treated as socially significant. The comparison here is with the Palazzo dei Congressi by Adalberto Libera. The space is compelled from end to end, but the ends become porticos. At the Palazzo dei

LEFT: Adalberto Libera, Palazzo dei Congressi, EUR, Rome, 1942; RIGHT: Foster Associates, The Sainsbury Centre, University of East Anglia, Norwich

Congressi this is made explicit by the way Libera was forced by Piacentini to place a colonnade of tuscan columns across the edge of the space. However, at what was thought of as the less important end, Libera was able to keep it clean, abstract and modern.

If we look more closely at these porticos, we find a further aspect which they share. Both make use of steel lattices – Sainsbury as main structure, dei Congressi as structural mullions to the windows. Steel lattice may be thought of as a token of modern construction: in each building this motif defines the same semantic space. This instance is not to be interpreted as imitation, but rather to demonstrate that over a certain period of architectural history latticed steel construction was not only structurally effective, but also *represented* modern construction. This is still the case, with so many contemporary buildings that use a glazed steel lattice to cover the 'atrium'. This is no relation to the Roman atrium, except that it too admitted light through a hole in the roof. The way that such spaces have become acceptable, even necessary, for the modern office structure as much as for the swimming pool, is itself instructive in illustrating the space of acceptance, the space in which a new convention arises to personify the future and simultaneously to perpetuate the past. Past and future are not alternatives, but components, in our cultural envelope.

LEFT: Palazzo dei Congressi, view across portico; RIGHT: The Sainsbury Centre, view across portico

The legend of Pandora's Box (actually her Jar)[24] is a potent one, one which expresses the modern quandary with much accurateness. Our curiosity has led us to question the mechanism of the universe, and we now see it as a sort of machine unwinding towards entropy. Gone is the reassuring sense that everything is accounted for by the mystery of the Godhead. Gone is the sense that belief and common sense tell the same story. During the Renaissance, European culture achieved a marvellous unity of expression. From the Enlightenment onwards, Man began to feel a stranger in the universe and a tourist in his own city. Piranesi's view of the Quirinale, from his *Vedute di Roma*, seems to represent this condition, in which we are never free of our past but can never return to it except as strangers. In a strictly scientific sense, we need our past in order to place ourselves within history and attempt to preview its future. There is, in cultural terms, no *tabula rasa*.

The achievements of science allow us to better understand how the mechanism of the universe works, and in the light of understanding, much that was solid in previous beliefs now seems to be illusion. The Post-Modern condition is not necessarily catastrophic – it is just that nothing is simple and easy any more, instead it is complex and fearful. However, if the jungle in which we live is a fearful place, it is better to know it. The orders of architecture have lost their mythical power, but we remember them with affection.

Piranesi, The Quirinale, *from* Vedute di Roma

GROWING UP IN GREAT BRITAIN

I have always had to fight to get things done. Fighting is my nature. In Britain, people are too absorbed in their history. There is an intense indulgence in the past. They won't accept that we have progressed since the Classical age, since the Greeks. There is an apprehension about new things. They can't mix old and new together.

Zaha Hadid, in an interview with Joanna Pitman
The Sunday Times, November 25, 1995

■ The polemic I have been advancing in this little book is directed at the cultural scene in Britain. I believe that we, in this country, remain curiously naïve about our culture, or more accurately, about what *culture* itself is and how it operates. We do not think of culture as the medium inside which we move and have our being, but as enclosing a separate category of 'cultural' things, to be referred to only in certain contexts (as when discussing literature) and not in others. We want to believe that we are free within nature, that in all things we relate immediately to nature, and that our experience of nature is direct and unmediated. Nikolaus Pevsner spoke of 'the English love of real and actual things'. Weekends in the Lake District are never seen as a cultural experience, but as something more immediate: sheer physical exercise, a relaxing interval, a social opportunity, or whatever. Sailing is a national sport because it pits us against the elements. And Cup Finals are experienced as the forces of nature in collision, not as cultural events. It took an American, TS Eliot, to point out the ritualistic content in his list of typically English things and to suggest that these are part of our lived religion. It took another American, Peter Eisenman, to point out the ironies and conceits in Stirling and Gowan's Leicester Engineering

Building, which the rest of us saw as a chunk of technological muscle.

In Britain there is a deep-seated attitude towards all philosophical questions that might cloud the immediacy of actuality. It is an attitude that fundamentally sees them as part of talk, and not of action, and therefore doomed to be inconsequential and easy to dismiss. We come back to the famous *bon mot* of Dr Samuel Johnson, who, listening to an argument that he did not much like, answered: 'Sir, I refute you thus', kicking out of the way a stone that lay in his path. This down-to-earth response is characteristic of the British empirical tradition. In the hard sciences it has been hugely successful, with its systematic use of the 'empirical test' as a way of refuting hypotheses, including interesting ones. Isaac Newton inveighed against hypothesis-making, which he regarded as a Continental trick. He was unaware of the hypotheses that underlay his own thinking. Karl Popper's emphasis on the process of refutation, as the only way for science to advance, was of a piece with his settling in Britain, where the empirical tradition is not regarded as a tradition. The more interesting the hypothesis, the more seductive it is, the more it needs to be refuted in the name of a higher principle. The higher principle is necessity, in the sense of following natural law, of not being willed, but completely independent of our thinking process. All other evidence built up by science fits together because it is. There is a physical reality 'out there', and it does not lend itself readily to our desires, but resists them, so bringing us back to our senses.

In Britain the paradigm for science is applied to all the arts, and the methodology of the portrait-maker provides a literal model of the artist's activity. It is not clear to me whether this literalness *is* naïvety, or a sort of puritanism. The latter idea is often advanced to explain why we are inclined to be hardhearted about the arts. Yet the huge popularity of art, as measured by the attendances at the Royal Academy Summer Show, would suggest that we love art. The Prince of Wales not only hunts and shoots but 'does' watercolours. And Churchill painted assiduously, if not very well, for recreation. Our theatre is big on Broadway, and gathers awards. Our sense of street fashion in London is far freer and less orthodox than the high fashion of Paris. And we are generally acknowledged to be superb at national ceremonial – royal marriages, fly-pasts, military tattoos, state banquets – in which everyone participating is strictly amateur, but extremely well *drilled*. And Francis Bacon (to our considerable discomfort, one suspects) is celebrated in the world as one of the great modern painters. We contribute to the cultural scene, so why complain about our hang-ups? Besides, if our attitude, as opposed to our performance, is odd, is this really due to our puritanism, or is it something else?

There is something odd about our attitude towards the past, I think. We like familiar things, but we also like freshness, new versions of the past. The art displayed in the Summer Show is strangely familiar, even when the paint is scarcely dry. It is familiar because of the almost unconscious way it reflects the history of painting over the last hundred years or so, and sometimes with considerable verve. There is always the trace of an accepted new master in the background: sometimes we see Cézanne, sometimes Gauguin, sometimes Matisse, sometimes Van Gogh, sometimes even Léger or Roy Lichtenstein, and so on. All of these were innovators in their time, but they are innovators that have since become thoroughly familiar, can be possessed through postcards and posters, and generally treated as pets. They are now part of the popular idea of what art is. They allow a sense of being in the know, of participating in 'modern' art, as opposed to measuring ourselves against the great tradition, which is impossibly remote.

The result in terms of the Summer Show is highly derivative, and it seems reasonable to conclude that the most important function of this truly popular art is not only to look pretty, but to be reassuring. Year after year, the re-cycling continues. And this, perhaps, could be taken as evidence for the existence of what I have called *The Animated Archive* – that bottomless bran tub in which everything that has ever been becomes something that can be re-used in a fresh way – with or without a touch of genius.

However, it *could* be naïvety, a refusal of the terms of life. It could mean simply that the existence of the cultural reservoir is denied, through the act of denying culture itself; but it could also point to a peculiarly British view of art as something nice that looks fresh but stays familiar, clouding the extent to which it welcomes the reiteration of an earlier innovation, that by now has lost its shock and become accepted. This seems to involve the adoption of a special standard – the standard of the gifted amateur – as more worthy, more sporting, and more sincere, than the work of the serious artist. The great thing would be to understate, to avoid pretension, to be not overly serious. The innovative architect Zaha Hadid has said of the British: 'There is an intense indulgence in the past . . . There is an apprehension about new things. They can't mix old and new together'. It may be more true to say that they cannot distinguish between old and new innovation. The Royal Academy Summer Show seems to work within the public's view of art as something fresh that stays nice, however shocking it may have been in the past. This attitude has become the target for the Turner Prize choices, which are clearly designed to inure the British public to shock, and to re-instate in the public mind the idea that 'real' art *must* be shocking.

This in turn brings up an interesting question about the relationship between the different arts, and the possibility that, in Britain, the arts of theatre and dance – the performance arts – are not so hidebound as the visual arts, since we seem to do them better. If this is in some measure true, I like to think that it goes back to the aristocracy's enjoyment of charades, amateur acting, and even schoolboyish transvestism, as appropriate activities to pass the tedium of country house weekends – good fun because strictly amateur. (It seems all right that Inigo Jones and Sir John Vanbrugh designed for the theatre before they went on to build palaces: in a way this suggests that they were gifted amateurs in architecture rather than serious thinkers.) Or it may mean that literature is somehow accepted here as the real mistress of the arts, and therefore uniquely privileged ever since Shakespeare. We always enjoy new productions of Shakespeare that bring him up to date by linking him to a current fad or fashion. It is true that our successful playwrights seem to have an instinct for what will prove to be a success with a West End audience, and that London is more famous for excessively long runs than for extremely short ones: that may simply speak to the dominance of theatre management in the trade. It is also true that, among key innovators of Modernism, neither James Joyce nor Samuel Beckett found an appreciative audience in Britain, and preferred exile on the Continent to a life in London. And Le Corbusier, although awarded the RIBA Gold Medal, was never given the opportunity to build in Britain.

However this may be, it seems the British public is very nervous about the idea that architecture could also be regarded as an art. The playwright takes his chance with the mood of the audience; if the play does not succeed, it is taken off and something more acceptable replaces it. Music that we do not like, we do not have to listen to. A painting that we do not like, we do not have to buy. Whereas a building that we do not like is probably going to be around for some time, so its degree of success or failure is not to be measured by the applause ratings. The architect is probably seen as unduly privileged, overly protected against public judgement in a situation where his work is going to be on display for a considerable time. Besides, there seems to be a reluctance to classify as art a professional activity that is supposed to lead to satisfied clients. The client pays good money up front for something that is expected to have a useful life; there is a reluctance to think of this money as a reward for the architect's self-expression. Self-expression is too close to self-indulgence.

This attitude is compounded by the modern architect's usual insistence that his building is not only the product of a professional service, but is based on empirical science, not arbitrary at all but the result of a total understanding of the situation:

that, as we have suggested, is the functionalist myth. Myth or not, it is impossible for the architect not to call on functional performance as the basis of his work. When Sir Denys Lasdun protests against the demolition of one of the terraces at the National Theatre, and points to the importance of this element as part of the compositional balance ('no-one would suggest demolishing a part of St Paul's cathedral') there is an uneasy suspicion that, all along, the architect did indeed regard his work as a composition, and therefore as art. It is noticeable that very successful architects do not stress this side of their work, preferring to present it as visionary, forward looking, ahead of the times, rather than as self-expression, or in any way an expression of the condition of society.

This reticence we may see as a stage in the expansion of the Modern Movement from being an élite movement of the avant-garde to being the common way of building for an industrialised society. Moshe Safdie made just such a claim for his large apartment complex – Habitat – build at the Montreal EXPO of 1967: he saw it as a movement of architecture towards economic reality, where large factory-made units would be assembled on the site. In fact, instead of being rationally assembled in straight lines, they were put together higgeldy-piggeldy so as to look as if they could be moved around, as if they were the accidental result of vernacular immediacy. This proved to be a complex operation, and very expensive. He called it 'a vernacular for our industrial society'.[25] But this version of the new Brutalist style, claiming to be universal, also moved architecture towards a deeper deception, hiding artistic intentions behind a show of following necessity. In the sixties 'necessity' shifted from being seen as something clean, geometric and rational to being something varied, organic and intuitive. Whether it is rational or intuitive, it continues to dissemble an intentionality close to artistic pretension. The straight artist did not dissemble to this extent, he did not wish to disown his responsibility for the result, but to gain credit for it. The architect was entangled in conceit, he wanted to disown artistic responsibility and claim that his results were, somehow, inevitable, the uncovering of forces in nature that could not be gainsaid. This is why ordinary people are inclined to be suspicious of architects, and who can blame them?

The scepticism of the public is not unreasonable on several counts. If architecture is about expression, it is undoubtedly an expensive way of seeking that outlet. If it is a form of dance, it is a somewhat elephantine one. The ancients were careful not to accord it the status of fine art, which had the duty of representing the myths and history of mankind, in order to celebrate his identity. Architecture, as Aristotle ruled, is a useful art – important as the site of the sculpture that most monumentally expressed the important myths, but essentially not a fine art; more properly, not an art, but a craft.

The growth of the modern social sciences has changed our view of what is fine and what is coarse. In the age of the Museum, we think it proper that a civilisation should be represented by *all* its artefacts: temple paintings and pyramids are equally important in defining the 'Egypt' of the museums, and both of these were allocated a task within that society. Since Burckhardt's massive study of the Italian Renaissance, we have a new concept of the way a civilisation can be imbued with a unique spirit of discovery, a realisation that soon leads on to the idea of cultural history. Anthropology has broadened our concept of the way any culture finds expression through its artefacts; modern psychology has shown that almost any artefact can be given a role as representative; the Saussurian 'science' of semiology has gone on to adumbrate the floating nature of language within the society of speakers, and the self-referential nature of all communicating systems. All these new areas of study, in which *critical theory* and *hermeneutics* are located, have redefined modernity, and brought us to the point where critics speak of the 'post-modern condition' as imposing an inescapable limit on the practical application of logical thought.

These developments are important for thinkers and intellectuals, but they hardly make an impact on the day-to-day conduct of affairs, especially in Britain. The radical artist is sensitive to these doubts and seeks to express them in work that tries to reveal or anticipate changes in the moral climate. If modern architecture is to be part of the radical activity of the avant-garde, it will want to be part of this world of expression. If it is primarily a craft, it will want to plead necessity and accept the judgement of ordinary people. These two points of view are in principle opposed but many young architects wish to somehow combine them, gaining satisfied clientele and an increase in work, but also succeeding as avant-garde artists before a narrower public.

This contradiction provides a very good explanation, I think, for the popularity of the High Tech style in Britain. Although forward looking, it is also well defined and complete. It is based on competence, not on self-expression. It is therefore reassuring. It has been, and continues to be, the accepted framework for enlightened patronage. Its key practitioners, who already constitute the architectural establishment, are all knighted or about to become so. They do not present their work as art, nor as composition, but as purely pragmatic, severely practical, especially geared to needs, liberating and Good for People. It is innovative too, but only because it is visionary, forward looking, ahead of the times. It is never presented as self-expression or as any kind of emotional reaction to the ambiguous condition of society.

In the British response to architecture considered as art, there is a strong moral reprobation of an art that is practised for the benefit of a professional career but paid for by the client. This moralism looks with suspicion on any kind of building that is not understood as a practical answer to practical problems. As a result, British architects tend to identify very strongly with the ideal of a technically competent architecture, where everything special about the design can be justified as the result of practical considerations, and never attributed to anything as inherently arbitrary as an artistic impulse. To avow artistic intentions in architecture is certain to arouse suspicion that the architect intends to make free with the client's money for his own purposes. Artistic intentions, if they exist, have to be dissimulated, and so a certain hypocrisy is introduced.

The High Tech style is about selling architecture as the acceptable face of the future. It is forward looking, but familiar.[26] If it is innovative, it is because technology innovates by adopting the empirical method of science, exploring natural frontiers, not cultural ones. There is nothing personal in it, you understand. It is not part of 'expression' at all, certainly not looking to express anything strange or fearful, except in the way that large structures can be impressive and good-looking, like suspension bridges, or elegant and strangely powerful, like gliders. The model for this behaviour was laid down during World War I by Le Corbusier, who claimed that engineering design showed architects the way. The High Tech school, so successful as establishment architecture in England today, is undoubtedly based on an extension of the functionalist approach that Le Corbusier promoted so energetically. Architecture is to be judged by its external relations, not by its inward connections.

If the High Tech school looks to the future for its justification, the Classical Revivalist school looks to the past. The British are proud of their past, seeing it perhaps as safely locked away. Stately homes open to the public are viewed with satisfaction by large numbers of people.[27] They show us who we were, and it was not inconsiderable. What were once bold or discreditable events are now written safely into the records. What were crimes are now colourful details. It was all once upon a time. Because our past seems greater than our present, we are inclined to be indulgent about it, as Zaha Hadid claims.

The architect practising Classical architecture does not arouse any paranoia against the self-indulgence of the architect masquerading as artist. Classical architecture is not seen as having anything to do with expression, but as following well defined rules. There are two sets of rules and they overlap without calling up any philosophical doubts about ends and means.

First, the canon of the Orders is a system of reproduction, not an excuse for innovation. Second, the technology appropriate to Classical buildings is the traditional one combining common sense and careful craftsmanship. Behind these principles is the sense of propriety peculiar to an architecture long sanctioned by the class structure. Only important buildings are entitled to deploy the orders *in extensio*. Most should be background buildings, providing scenic support, and, of course, should be reassuringly familiar. Propriety leads to a concept of appropriateness. The architect should not be too forward, should not proclaim himself as genius, still less as leader. Like the stiff upper lip, modesty is thought of as a typically British characteristic, leaving any distinction achieved to be determined by the civil service and rewarded in the appropriate Honours list. Thus the Classical Revivalists are able to protect or conceal any artistic intentions by presenting them as the incidental result of following an age-old technical tradition, one confirmed by centuries of use and enjoyment.

In a strange way, therefore, British architecture tends to polarise into two opposing camps, both of which rely on a technical argument and reject any idea of a free artistic impulse. On the one hand, the High Tech school advocates technical innovation and the use of new materials and techniques that may involve risk but will be seen as progressive. Architecture should be something up-to-date, equal to the modern world of lasers and computers, and the architect worth his salt absorbs the risk into his insurance policy. On the other hand, say the traditionalists, architecture is embodied in buildings that have to join up with existing buildings to knit the environment together. No one building should be excessively experimental, or award itself a peculiar status. Prince Charles has championed the cause of a traditional architecture that works because it follows well-tried and tested methods, and avoids unnecessary risk altogether. In both cases, we may note, it is a practical argument that is emphasised, and personal expression that is played down.

Moreover, each of these attitudes is thought of as already fixed in operation and in result. With each of these, you can anticipate the outcome of the trauma of commissioning, you know broadly what you will get: it will be pleasantly fresh and at the same time familiar, like strawberries at Wimbledon. Each one of these schools of thought takes on the aura of your favourite football team, and feelings of loyalty add to the pleasure of choosing between them, like joining the right club. The aim of adopting these broad stylistic categories must be to circumscribe the architect and prescribe in advance the result that will be acceptable. For the architect who wishes to profit from this (entering into the very complicity deplored by Roland Barthes),[28] the right behaviour to adopt is a becoming modesty, providing, of course, that he is thoroughly sure of his own competence and can guarantee the results. No wonder Zaha has trouble: she is a tempestuous artist who knows exactly what feelings she wants to express, feelings about the future, not as technological prowess but as abstract art, feelings about its strangeness and its flux. Modesty does not come into it.

The actuality is that architects who privately intend to make art behave exactly like other artists: the degree of modesty or boldness they assume is nicely judged in relation to what they think they can get away with. Architects have no doubts, when talking amongst themselves, that originality is a large part of what makes the career worthwhile. Those who are in the game only for the money – and this means the great majority of 'commercial' architects – are despised by the real movers. If architecture was always determined by function and economy, it would tend towards an anonymous uniformity, yet in practice it betrays considerable variety from one country to another and from one designer to another. To the extent that the physical determinants are important, they are already varied by different cultural components. To the extent that each case is unique, it is already contaminated by cultural universals.

Among the cultural determinants is the concept of style. Style evolves from the distinctive manner of the individual and becomes the property of the group. The International Style was virtually the invention of Le Corbusier, with a little help from Philip Johnson.[29] Style generalises particular qualities just as the concept of type generalises buildings of similar use. Type and style are known before the particular outcome. We design *in* a style as we speak *in* a language. To choose a style in which to design is a way of limiting the outcome, so as to encompass the unknown.

For the individual designer, the establishment of a style is a crucial step in the process of becoming recognised as occupying a niche in the culture of design. The international stars like Richard Meier and Frank Gehry are admired for their verve and *chutzpah*, but they are also, to some extent, governed by the conception of style as a way of identifying their work in the market place. Meier is known for his 'modernity', Gehry for his 'unorthodoxy'. Each has taken risks, then consolidated his approach.

To the degree that each has developed his own personal style, these architects have become recognisable and to an extent 'safe'. The style of each is by now a marketable commodity and in commissioning one of them, you already know what you will get. This is not essentially different from the way that any artist achieves social recognition and gets to occupy a niche. The poet appointed Poet Laureate is expected to produce occasional

LEFT: Richard Meier, The High Museum, Atlanta, Georgia;
RIGHT: Frank Gehry, The Guggenheim Museum, Bilbao, maquette

verse appropriate to particular occasions; he was chosen for his style and will be recognised for his style, as much as for his preferred subjects. In commissioning Lucian Freud or Francis Bacon to paint a portrait, you knew in advance what you were undertaking. Both these artists went through a long period during which they were developing their personal style, not at all to function as a market label, but in the course of a personal quest for expression. When they have explored their language and can communicate powerfully within it, they will achieve recognition. Within the art of architecture, where this public status has not yet been achieved, the architect too is embarked on his own personal odyssey.

In 1975, Elia Zenghelis proposed a fantastic building – The Hotel Sphinx – for a site in Manhattan at the site of Broadway and Seventh Avenue. Although it straddles a street, it is perfectly practicable as an intervention in the city. It recognises the pattern of streets and occupies a designated plot. It does not demand a *tabula rasa* or a mountain top. This project demonstrates that fantasy can be effective within strict limits. By its sensitive combination of abstract and representational forms, it is capable of being legible within the framework of the city. As the trace of a certain sensibility, The Hotel Sphinx is original and innovative, defining a possibility that has not yet become a public category but is still a remarkable personal achievement.

Elia Zenghelis, project for The Hotel Sphinx, Manhattan

In more general terms, it undoubtedly confirms the status of architecture as a system of expression, as an art.

For it is an art. To deny it this status, at least as a potential, is to deny it retrospectively its important place in culture and in the history of a community. The denial of it as art has created problems of understanding, compounded by the hypocrisy that wishes to avoid outright condemnation of artistic pretensions. There, too, Zaha Hadid's behaviour has been exemplary, devoid of false modesty and dissimulation. She declares her aims in no uncertain terms, claiming the high ground, 'coming out' for her art.

For too long the myths of Function and Space have dominated. They were once part of an excitement about modernity and the twentieth century. They were a projection of what was for the most part a socialist ideology, anticipating the liberation of mankind from ancient tyrannies, and the betterment of social conditions through rational analysis. Increasingly it is obvious that the kind of world envisaged in the twenties and thirties is not the world that has come about. The human animal continues to behave in a completely irrational way and evil is as widespread as it ever was. To contemplate the plethora of benches, standard lamps and planting boxes in the public spaces of Toulouse-le-Mirail[30] is to realise the absurd hopes that were pinned by modern architects on the idea that good design could purify the environment and restore virtue. We are far from living in a rational utopia; with the advent of television, cybernetics and virtual reality, our life style is increasingly compounded of fantasy, a fantasy that is shared and that has ominous similarities with group madness. The philosophical questions are beginning to seem more important, and the recovery of an ethical perspective more urgent than fifty years ago. Is it not time that Britain abandoned simplistic codes of behaviour and joined the moral universe?

The physical prowess beloved by the High Tech experts looks increasingly like games with the Meccano set. The excruciating properness of the Classical Revivalists seems increasingly like Establishmentarianism. We should let them do what they want, both approaches can be done well or badly, but neither should be given the accolade of orthodoxy. It is more important that quality should be secreted within the shell of the building, in whatever style it is conceived, than that any 'side' should win. It is not a question of laying down the law, but of opening up possibilities. There are many more possibilities than are encompassed by this deadening polarity.

Hannes Meyer perpetuated the problem by insisting first that architecture was not an art, and then, that if it was an art, it was purely through its capacity as an organising principle. It was *nothing but* the product of *Function* and *Economy*. He wrote it as an equation: *Function x Economy*, thus enclosing it in a tight formula, with the outcome pre-determined. Given that Gropius spread a similar, if looser, doctrine to the West, extolling group work as a way of avoiding eccentricity, this formula excluded the very possibility of personal expression. It confirmed the objectivist position across both political camps. The Vitruvian trinity of *Commodity, Firmness, Delight* is by comparison innocuous, a mere shopping list, less doctrinaire, more democratic. It implies no unique relationship between the elements, but a variable composition.

What was originally doctrine has become PR. No architect is going to deny the claims of Commodity and Firmness, in modern terms Space and Structure. Satisfaction on these counts is expected from a professional service. However, to believe that proper attention to them automatically ensures Delight, is a fiction. If the result is to include Delight, it is up to the architect to put Delight into the pot. If his Delight is of the kind that comes only with elegant structure and free space, no one will complain if he delivers functional efficiency as well. If his search is for a poetics of architecture, he can be reticent about it, but he should not lie about it. Denying an artistic intent will not automatically protect him from the risks of attempting it.

We all have our preferences and my own are no better than those proposed by anyone else, but I should state them here.

LEFT: Tadao Ando, House, 1988, interstitial space; CENTRE: Chipperfield Architects, Graphics Studio, Brownlow Mews, London, 1987; RIGHT: Nicholas Grimshaw, Euro Terminal, Waterloo, London

Typically British as I am, I prefer the understated to the overblown. Typically provincial as I am, I prefer the personal to the institutional. The qualities that move me occur in the interstices of a building, when I can recognise, within the empirical necessity, a sensibility at work: the trace of an emotion felt and registered. I find this in many kinds of design, originating from many different schools. The style, whether received or adumbrated, is but a vehicle for this moment of emotion, which can obliquely approach the sense of a truth. It is interesting, for example, that the heightened sense of space can strike home on the convex side of a curve that encloses space, as in these two examples produced at almost the same moment, from opposite sides of the world; examples, incidentally, which show that architectural culture is fast approaching the era of global warming: one world, one human condition.

Whatever the claims that can be made for its functionality, its rationality, the sensation of emerging from EuroStar into Nick Grimshaw's Terminal building is one of confronting sheer beauty, and if the architect is too modest to admit that he tried to achieve that beauty, the critic must ascribe it to him. This example also provides evidence that the High Tech style is itself in movement, shifting away from pseudo-rationalism towards a more expressive goal.

When the main lines of the Modern style were created by Le Corbusier in the twenties, a rationalist expression was preferred. It felt clean, it looked efficient and it made it easier to claim the mantle of the scientist and argue that necessity, not expression, was the *raison d'être* of architectural design. After three-quarters of a century, that idea has run its course. The current interest in the utopian fantasies of the Russian Constructivists heralds a return to expression. In terms of style, it is a form of expressionism, but not a return, exactly, to the expressionism of the twenties or the *Neue Sachlichkeit* of the thirties. The conceptual thinking that was introduced by Duchamp has had a profound effect on all the arts, including architecture conceived as art, and this ingredient changes the way the archive is animated today. It is another moment, and every moment has its day.

At the élite level this effervescence reveals itself in experiments with hybrid forms and the play of abstraction, often based on the transfer of art forms into building forms. At the popular level, it reveals itself as a preference for the over-stated, the obvious – as with the concept of the Glass Cathedral, or architecture as a Glass Wave. It is a sad fact that similar ideas expressed as graphic gestures, as with Bruno Taut, for example, were once inspiring; built, seventy years later, the effect of the built reality is at first impressive, but then disappointing. To apply the words of Auden: *Art in intention is Mimesis / But realized, the resemblance ceases* . . . The over-simplification, the banality of such ideas, once built, in spite of their popular appeal, is another good reason for looking for a more thoughtful form of modern architecture: an architecture that can open the inner eye, restore a faith in inwardness. This does not mean abandonment of the Modern tradition. The rationalist forms of the heroic period are capable of being reconsidered, taken into meditation, allowed to speak with irony and so project an awareness of the human condition and of its fragile grasp on values. This is precisely the achievement of Stirling in the Braun factory. Such projects can create a depth where there was only surface, and suggest a future that has not yet been institutionalised and that could, once again, encourage hope.

Meantime, it is interesting to note that the graphic fantasies of the thirties are capable of inspiring a virtual reality for today. The special effects which can make dinosaurs run amongst people and alien life forms burst out of human bodies also allow the actual construction of ideas that were originally only graphic gestures on a two dimensional plane. Build a three-dimensional model of Duchamp's *Bride Descending a Staircase* and you have effectively created a piece of 'deconstructive' architecture *à la* Coop Himmelblau. Fisher-Park's demountable set for the Rolling Stones World Tour is a moveable feast, reconstituted in new settings that are always the same: strobe lights, heavy noise, heaving bodies. Its forms are directly inspired by a fantasy of Chernikov. If architecture for popular consumption can be so erudite, when are our 'serious' architects going to extend the range of their inspiration?

LEFT: Chernikov, architectural fantasy, 1930; RIGHT: Fisher-Park, demountable stage for the Rolling Stones, 1994

NOTES

1 Francis Bacon spoke of a condition of 'exhilarated despair', David Sylvester, *Interviews with Francis Bacon*, Thames & Hudson, London, 1975, p66.
2 Karl Popper, *The Poverty of Historicism*, Routledge & Kegan Paul, London, 1961.
3 Georg Simmel, *On Individuality and Social Forms*, University of Chicago Press, Chicago & London, 1971, p391.
4 Emilio Ambasz, in a lecture given at the School of Architecture, Princeton University, Princeton, October 1967.
5 Robert Maxwell, *Sweet Disorder and the Carefully Careless*, Princeton Architectural Press, New York, 1993.
6 See particularly Jacques Derrida, *De la grammatologie*, English Edition trans Gayatri Spivak, Johns Hopkins, Baltimore, 1974.
7 Gianni Vattimo, *The End of Modernity*, trans Snyder, Johns Hopkins, Baltimore, 1988.
8 TS Eliot, *Notes Towards a Theory of Culture*, Faber & Faber, London, 1948.
9 Ibid.
10 Raymond Williams, *Culture*, Fontana, Glasgow, 1981.
11 Ernst Gombrich, *In Search of Cultural History*, Oxford University Press, London, 1969.
12 See Roland Barthes, *Mythologies*, Editions du Seuil, Paris, 1957.
13 See Adolf Loos, *Spoken into the Void*, trans Newman, MIT Press, Cambridge (MA) and London, 1982.
14 WR Lethaby, *Form in Civilisation*, Oxford University Press, London, 1922; D'Arcy Thompson, *On Growth and Form*, (1914) Cambridge University Press, London and New York, 1961.
15 When my neighbour, the artist Gwen Barnard, visited the Pompidou Centre soon after it opened, she was thrilled: 'It was like seeing the future'. She was over 70 at the time.
16 Op cit, Roland Barthes.
17 It was Reyner Banham who spoke of the 'cultural load' that the artist must shed if he wished to keep pace with technology. *Theory and Design in the First Machine Age*, The Architectural Press, London, 1960, p330.
18 Robert Maxwell, in a lecture *The Animated Archive*, given as Graduation

Day Address at the School of Architecture, University of Manitoba, Winnipeg, May 1986.
19 Many critics believe that the Sainsbury Extension at the National Gallery in London is a work of classical pastiche, because it has a cluster of imitated Corinthian columns adjacent to the entrance. It is hard to imagine a building less given to a classical parti. The plan, if it owes to anyone, owes to Aalto, and Aalto never hesitated to enrich the area around the entrance, as with the differentiation of materials he employs at the Alajäri Town Hall and the Library at the Otaniemi Institute of Technology. Venturi intended the cluster of columns to be in a sort of 'jazz' rhythm, deliberately a populist comment, not a piece of serious pastiche (in a conversation, June 1993).
20 Demetri Porphyrios (ed), *Classicism is not a Style*, Academy Editions, London, 1982.
21 Francis Fukuyama, *The End of History*, Penguin, London, 1992.
22 The United States Government recently granted a patent to a method of mutating genes.
23 A remark of the Director, Georg Braun, at the official opening of the building at Melsungen on 26 May 1995.
24 Froma Zeitlin, in a lecture at Princeton University, 16 November 1992.
25 Moshe Safdie, in a lecture at Princeton University, October 1971.
26 See note 15.
27 'I sometimes think, when I contemplate England – where I grew up – that the prevailing religion is a kind of domesticated pantheism: a communion with shrubberies and rockeries, with the song thrush at the birdbath, with the look in the eye of a reliable well-behaved dog. Even the landscape seems to have been moulded into a paradisial national theme park. Great masses of British tourists tramp through places of natural beauty the way people in Chaucer's day used to visit Christian shrines', Kennedy Fraser, 'Straying from the Way', *The New Yorker*, 4 December 1995.
28 Op cit, Roland Barthes.
29 Philip Johnson and Henry-Russell Hitchcock, in their defining book *The International Style*, 1932, made Le Corbusier the key figure. The 1966 edition (Norton) had a picture of Le Corbusier's *Villa Savoye* on the cover.
30 Toulouse-le-Mirail, an urban extension by Candilis and Woods, is probably the largest and most comprehensive 'modern' environment ever built.